Unilateral Acts

We are in a moment where peoples and states are interested, directly or indirectly, in asserting their "national interest," unilaterally if necessary. In the White House, the national security policy is premised on "America First," while Catalans and Iraqi Kurds have taken steps to unilaterally declare their independence. All of these actions have generated tension both domestically and internationally. However, even though the potential for unilateral action has been receiving a lot of attention, the larger issue of the legality of unilateral acts is often hard to discern. This book provides a history of the doctrine of unilateral acts in international law, tracing their treatment in the international sphere from consent-based acts, to obligations *erga omnes*, to acts of estoppel.

Through chapter-by-chapter case studies, this book traces the "legalization" of the category of unilateral acts from its nineteenth-century foundations into a broad category of obligation. To understand why and how this occurred, this book examines the history of the legal doctrine of unilateral acts, which shows that in spite of efforts to progressively make unilateral acts "legal" they are still not precisely defined or easy to apply, challenging the very commitment these acts are meant to establish.

Betina Appel Kuzmarov is an Assistant Professor in the Department of Law and Legal Studies and Associate Dean (Students and Enrolment) in the Faculty of Public Affairs at Carleton University, Ottawa, Ontario, Canada (currently on leave).

Routledge Research in International Law

Available:

The Rule of Unwritten International Law
Customary Law, General Principles, and World Order
Peter G. Staubach

State Interest and the Sources of International Law
Doctrine, Morality, and Non-Treaty Law
Markus P. Beham

Demilitarisation and International Law in Context
The Åland Islands
Sia Spiliopoulou Åkermark and Saila Heinikoski

International Criminal Law and Sexual Violence against Women
The Interpretation of Gender in the Contemporary International Criminal Trial
Daniela Nadj

Unilateral Acts
A History of a Legal Doctrine
Betina Appel Kuzmarov

Regional Developmentalism Through Law
The Use of Law to Support the Effective Establishment of an African Economic Community
Jonathan Bashi Rudahindwa

China's One Belt One Road Initiative and Private International Law
Poomintr Sooksripaisarnkit and Sai Ramani Garimella

For a full list of titles in this series, visit www.routledge.com/Routledge-Research-in-International-Law/book-series/INTNLLAW

Unilateral Acts

A History of a Legal Doctrine

Betina Appel Kuzmarov

Routledge
Taylor & Francis Group
LONDON AND NEW YORK

First published 2018 by Routledge

2 Park Square, Milton Park, Abingdon, Oxfordshire OX14 4RN
52 Vanderbilt Avenue, New York, NY 10017

Routledge is an imprint of the Taylor & Francis Group, an informa business

First issued in paperback 2020

British Library Cataloguing-in-Publication Data
A catalogue record for this book is available from the British Library

Library of Congress Cataloging-in-Publication Data
Names: Kuzmarov, Betina, 1975-
Title: Unilateral acts : a history of a legal doctrine/Betina Appel Kuzmarov.
Description: Abingdon, Oxon ; New York, NY : Routledge, 2018. | Series Routledge research in international law
Identifiers: LCCN 2018006422 | ISBN 9781138060180 (hardback)
Subjects: LCSH: Unilateral acts (International law)
Classification: LCC KZ1262.J87 K89 2018 | DDC 341.26—dc23
LC record available at https://lccn.loc.gov/2018006422

ISBN: 978-1-138-06018-0 (hbk)
ISBN: 978-0-367-59038-3 (pbk)

Typeset in Galliard
by Apex CoVantage, LLC

For George and Ellie who made me who I am, for Sara who shows me who I am, for Ian who makes me better than I am, and for Ari who makes me all I am.

Contents

Preface

I was a wet-behind-the-ears PhD student at the Law School in Hull, UK, thinking of writing a thesis on international legal pluralism. It was late 2003, and the invasion of Iraq had been underway for months. There was a buzz in the legal community and it was about "unilateralism."

At the time, the term unilateralism was thrown around carelessly in general conversation. What did it mean and to whom did it apply? Was it the same as unilateral actions in international law? Dupuy has described unilateralism as "Like the God Janus of old, the notion seems to have two faces: one properly legal, the other more deliberately political" (Dupuy 2000, 20). And, in 2003 it seemed that the legal community was consumed with trying to understand this distinction. Legally it "denotes the taking of unilateral legal actions" that "express the will of only one subject. . . . Whether aimed at establishing . . . a legal position . . . establishing its sovereign rights . . . or creating legal commitments," whereas politically it refers to states using these unilateral acts to achieve a specific state aim (Dupuy 2000, 20). I am a lawyer by training and, knowing my limits, I decided to dig further into the legal aspect of unilateralism, unilateral acts of states. I got started with the research and writing process. As with most dissertations, my work morphed over time into something broader, and yet more focused, than my original impulse to investigate unilateralism. I became interested, some would say obsessed, with the theory and doctrine of unilateral acts. What was this tenuous category of legal obligation?

In this book, I examine the history of the doctrine of unilateral acts; specifically, I examine how these acts came to be legally regulated and the doctrinal explanations of their legality. In this book, I focus on the various attempts by international lawyers and international institutions to formulate when and how these acts would have legal implications. At this point, you may be asking yourself why, if you are not getting the "sexy" politics of unilateralism, why should you read or buy a book on unilateral acts? I can give you no better answer than the experts of the International Law Commission

(ILC) who worked on this topic from 1996–2006. They decided to include this topic on their agenda because,

> In their conduct in the international sphere, States frequently carry out unilateral acts with the intent to produce legal effects. The significance of such unilateral acts is constantly growing as a result of the rapid political, economic and technological changes taking place in the international community at the present time and, in particular, the great advances in the means for expressing and transmitting the attitudes and conduct of States;
>
> (Report of the International Law Commission on the Work of its Forty-Ninth Session (1997), 2)

Cutting through the bureaucratic language, the ILC offers a compelling reason for gaining greater understanding of unilateral acts; they are very common in international law and are becoming more common. They are fundamental building blocks of international law. However, they are not very well understood. As this book will show, until the nineteenth century unilateral acts were not categorically considered part of international law and, other than in certain limited circumstances, they were relegated to the political sphere. Anyone interested in international law or international relations, particularly those readers who are academics, students, or policy makers will be confronted with these acts. By gaining a thorough understanding of these acts readers will also gain insight into the history of the "legalization" of international relations.

You may also be wondering why this book is important now. As the ILC also noted, these acts are becoming increasingly pervasive. In the past year alone there have been several important unilateral acts. For example, Kurds and Catalans have moved unilaterally (although not without tension) to declare independence and the United States under President Trump has made it official national security policy to "put America first" in the "national" interest (National Security Strategy of the United States of America (December 2017) 2017; Zucchono 2017; Stone 2017). The range of these acts includes, but is much broader than, unilateral military action such as the invasion of Iraq (whether in self-defence or not) or declarations of independence. It can include action on the environment, trade, or any of the other multifaceted ways that states interact on a daily basis. As a result, it is increasingly important to understand how these acts operate today, and one important way to do this is by examining the history of the doctrine of unilateral acts. This book fills this gap.

In fact, examining the doctrinal history of unilateral acts will show that the attempts to define and regulate these acts have been one example of the "legalization" of international politics. I will show that "legalizing" unilateral acts have been a continual challenge for international law. This leads me to conclude that it is not effective to try to maintain unilateral acts as a category of legal obligation within the doctrine. As a result, it is more practical to discuss individual forms of unilateral acts (such as promises) as obligations while considering the category of unilateral acts as a whole as one of the building blocks of international law.

So, with this background in mind, I invite you to join me in tracing the history of the doctrine of unilateral acts.

Acknowledgements

I would like to thank all those who made this book possible.

Professor Richard Barnes and Dr. Richard Burchill (formerly) of the Law School, The University of Hull who supervised my PhD dissertation, on which this book is based, deserve a special thank you for their patience and perseverance. I would also like to thank my examiners, Professor Susan Breau and Ms. Catherine Mitchell whose tough hand and solid feedback only made the project better. Additionally, I would like to thank my fellow students at the University of Hull who made this process worthwhile.

Since I came to Carleton University, I have had the support of many people including Professor George Rigakos, who as Chair of the Department of Law and Legal Studies (at the time) encouraged me to just "publish the book" and my colleagues, particularly Melanie Adrian, Kamari Clarke, Ummni Khan, Umut Oszu, and Barry Wright, who read my proposal or parts of drafts. Dean André Plourde who supported my research and Jay Ramasubramanyam for his excellent research assistance.

I must also acknowledge my parents, Ellie and George Kuzmarov, as well as my sister, Sara Kuzmarov. Without their support, the PhD dissertation that formed the heart of this book would not have been possible.

To my partner forever, Ian Appel, without your encouragement this book would never have been completed and to my joy, Ari, without you sleeping on me I never would have perfected one-handed typing.

Thanks!

1 Introduction

> Sovereignty, formalism, positivism, a rule of coexistence, rather than cooperation, all remain with us, not only as echoes and remnants to be exercised root and branch, but as dreams, projects, goals for our work.
>
> (D. Kennedy 1996, 388)

As Kennedy points out twenty-first century international law is heavily indebted to the doctrines of the nineteenth century. Unilateral acts were a part of the drive in that century to formalize international law and, as a result, to progressively make legal all acts that states undertake that have international effects. However, examining the history of the doctrine of unilateral acts also demonstrates how challenging it was when states tried to apply this doctrine to specific acts. As a result, I argue that it is not effective to try to maintain unilateral acts as a separate, unified category of legal obligation. Instead, I suggest, it is more important to discuss individual forms of unilateral acts (such as promises, notifications, or reservations) as obligations in international law while promoting a category of unilateral acts, acts undertaken by one state alone, as part of the foundational acts of international law.

What Is a Unilateral Act?

A basic definition of a unilateral act is any action a state undertakes without reference to another state (Dupuy 2000, 20). That is, any act a state does on its own, even if it has an effect on another state. Since this category is so broad, much of what is considered international law begins with unilateral acts. For example, promises are made, notices of actions taken are given, protests are lodged, reservations are made to treaties, optional declarations are made to treaties, new states are recognized (or not recognized), and new customs are tried as a unilateral action.

These acts have been fundamental to the practice of international relations. But, oddly, there is nothing in Dupuy's definition to explain why these acts are binding on states as law. The fact that these acts do not, on their face, contain a legal obligation makes it difficult to categorize these acts within international law. When a group of international experts under the auspices of the United Nations General Assembly (UNGA), the International Law Commission (ILC), worked on this topic from 1996–2006, they contributed a lot to systematizing the concept. But, they never reached an agreed upon definition of a unilateral act (Report of the International Law Commission on the Work of its Fifty-Eighth Session (2006) UN DOC A/61/10, Supplement 10 n.d.). In the end, they set out guidelines for unilateral acts. In these guidelines, they skilfully avoided the problem of delineating the category of unilateral acts. This is not a trivial shortcoming, as it makes it nearly impossible to meaningfully apply a general category of unilateral acts.

In fact, this shortcoming highlights two challenges that need to be addressed at the outset of any book on unilateral acts. The first challenge is how to set limits on the category of unilateral acts, in absence of a clear definition. The second challenge, which arises out the first, is understanding how unilateral acts relate to other acts such as unilateral declarations that are often included within this category of acts so that the terminology is often used interchangeably.

Saganek argues that there are two approaches that writers often take to limiting the category of unilateral acts. They either choose to define unilateral acts and then list the acts that fall into this category or they list the acts and then reach a general definition (Saganek 2015, 2). Problematically, as Eckhart notes (citing Fiedler 2000) and as was discussed above, if one takes the first approach there is no generally accepted definition of unilateral acts (Eckhart 2012, 18). This means that writers who take this approach are effectively substituting their own definition for a general definition of these obligations. One example of this problem came up when writing this book; there was no consensus among major international law textbooks about where these acts fit into the structure that forms the doctrine of international law. There was agreement that unilateral acts are a category of legal obligation, but what this meant was different for each author.

For example, Robert Jennings and Arthur Watts in *Oppenheim's International Law* placed the detailed discussion of unilateral acts in a chapter entitled "on international transactions in general" under a subheading "transactions besides negotiation and treaties." Ian Brownlie placed them in the chapter "Other transactions including agency and representation. On the other hand, Antonio Cassese discussed unilateral acts under his Part III "Creation and Implementation of International Legal Standards" in a chapter titled "other law-making processes" in a section headed "unilateral acts as sources of obligation." In contrast to these approaches Malcolm Shaw placed unilateral acts in his chapter on "sources." He considered these acts under the heading "Other possible sources of international law." And Hugh Thirlway discussed them as part of his discourse on how "new sources" could "come into existence (Jennings and Watts 1996, 1187ff; Brownlie 1998, 642ff; Cassese 2005,

184ff' Shaw 1997, 95ff; Thirlway 2010, 115ff). This book contributes to the scholarly debate over unilateral acts by adding a historical examination of these acts as a way of explaining this lack of doctrinal agreement. However, this work must ultimately accept the shortcoming of not having a widely agreed definition of the topic.

One possible reason the doctrine of unilateral acts has resisted definition is because the category of unilateral acts includes very different types of acts (Saganek citing Fiedler in (Saganek 2015, 9)). Thus, deriving unilateral acts from a list of acts it includes is problematic because one would have to arrive at an "exhaustive" list of acts. In spite of this, Saganek goes on to note, that unilateral acts usually include several "classic" acts: promise (or notification), waiver, recognition and protest (Saganek 2015, 2). However, this approach also has not yielded an agreed-upon list of unilateral acts. Further, it is not obvious that given the wide range of acts often included in this list a definition will be forthcoming. For example, a promise is a positive action, such as the State of Israel's promise to unilaterally withdraw from the Gaza strip. It said it would do so, and it acted on this promise in order to fulfil it. Waivers, recognition, and protest are also a positive action. However, one major category of unilateral act not included in this list is silence. Acquiescence (that is doing nothing, i.e. staying silent and allowing an act) is often included in discussions of unilateral acts and it is a non-action, such as, the *de facto* recognition by many states of Taiwan. It too is a necessary unilateral act, but what definition can encompass these classic acts as well as non-acts such as acquiescence? Only a broad definition such as Dupuy's can meet this challenge. This leads to the suggestion that the category of unilateral acts is so broad that it is ultimately ineffective; to use Abbot et al.'s terms it is impossible to delegate (Abbott, et al. 2000, 402ff), so that it might be more worthwhile for the doctrine to discuss specific forms of unilateral acts rather than the category as a whole.

In this book, unilateral acts refer to all the acts noted earlier as well as non-acts such as silence (acquiescence). In fact, given this work's unique historical approach, it will refrain from listing specific acts to be included, in favour of taking a contextual approach. Specifically, this book uses Dupuy's broad definition cited at the outset so that unilateral acts are any undertaken without reference to another state. The only limitation that is placed on this category is historical/contextual. Throughout this book these acts are defined by the doctrine as it was framed in the time and place under discussion. Anything further would produce anachronistic studies of these acts and would assume a false unity in the doctrine.

It is important to note that this lack of a clear definition has other problems that are associated with it. The most important of these was discussed previously, terminology. Often the term unilateral act of states has been used interchangeably with the term unilateral declaration (see the general discussion in (Eckhart 2012, 19–22). However, as Eckhart notes, a declaration implies a positive action, as he puts it "a public declaration 'manifesting the will to be bound'" (Eckhart 2012, 22) which in fact excludes acquiescence as an act (Eckhart 2012, 21). As such, the term is not broad enough for the purposes of this book, although the term unilateral acts will be used to include declarations and that terminology may be used to refer to unilateral acts when that is the accurate terminology in its historical context (for example, in the discussion of the *Nuclear Tests Cases* in Chapter 3).

There are challenges inherent in choosing not to define or list these acts. As Fassbender and Peters have written, "Writing a history on given subject depends on making innumerable choices. . . . What is important is that authors consciously reflect about the choices they make and are explicit and transparent about them" (Fassbender and Peters 2012, 15). So, while the lack of definition or clear taxonomy may be problematic for some readers, I cannot provide you with a comprehensive definition or list of unilateral acts. Instead, you will come away with a clear idea of how international actors have wrestled with these acts. To avoid the suggestion that this is begging the question at best (or sloppy at worst), this approach is most appropriate for an historical work as it allows the doctrine to speak for itself over time. It does, however, require close attention to terminology of unilateral acts, in order to provide structure and rigour to an otherwise general discussion.

One additional weakness of Dupuy's definition is that it assumes that it is easy to tell when an act is unilateral. In fact, it is not always clear when an act is unilateral or not. To use Abbot et al.'s terminology, the category is not precise (Abbott, et al. 2000, 402ff). For example, as Chapter 2 will discuss, one oft-cited example of a unilateral act, the *Eastern Greenland Case*, occurred in the course of negotiations and was subsequently raised during a Court case. Given that negotiations were the basis of the declaration at issue in the Court case, it makes sense to ask whether this was truly the act of one state without reference to another state. A further common example of a unilateral act arises with the first state to act on a new custom that it is subsequently followed by other states. The initial act is unilateral, but it is the reaction to the act by other states that becomes important to the assessment of the act itself. The lines become fuzzy when deciding whether the unilateral act is "truly" unilateral. As will be demonstrated, this lack of clarity has dogged unilateral acts since the nineteenth century.

In fact, I will demonstrate that, since the nineteenth century, there have been repeated attempts to clarify the nature of unilateral acts. One way to understand these attempts at definition are as repeated efforts to "legalize" unilateral acts. Legalization is the attempt to "institutionalize" these acts in a form that contains a "legally binding" commitment. To meet this standard, the commitment should be easily defined, that is "precise," and it must be capable of recognition, interpretation and application by third parties (Abbott, et al. 2000, 402). However, unilateral acts have resisted these attempts at legalization and, in fact, have not even been clearly defined.

Unilateral Acts and the History of International Law

The problems associated with defining and legalizing unilateral acts can be fully understood only in the context of the history of international law. A central premise is that the history of international law has presented itself as universal when, in fact, it is a distinctly European history that has been imposed on the non-European world. As a result, when historians have searched for the origins of this law it has usually had a Western focus, with Greece, Rome, and the Mediterranean often cited as the sources of modern international law. To put this in technical terms, the history of international law has usually been traced from the "law of nations" as it developed into "international law" in Europe and North America up to and after World War II (Yasuaki 2000, 55).

The transition from the older law of nations to modern international law has often been dated to 1648 with the signing of the treaties marking the Peace of Westphalia. These treaties were a series of agreements that ended the Thirty Years' War within the Holy Roman Empire, in what is modern-day Germany. It contained two primary treaties signed between the Empire and the Netherlands and Spain. Within international law these treaties have often been used to date the arrival of the concept of sovereign equality of States. From this starting point, international law's history has been portrayed as a story of progress, one that resulted in the extension of the European concept of statehood to all peoples, a process that has culminated in the decolonization movement post-World War II (Anghie 2006, 740).

This story of progress, however, only makes sense if international law is the product of a linear history from Europe to universality. In fact, the history of international law may be the product of at least two trends: One trend was the development of the idea of sovereign equality within Europe and the other was the process of the encounter between European sovereigns and non-European peoples and the way this encounter formed international law. A further trend is the regional and local customs amongst neighbours that have existed across the globe, which formed an alternate set of relations to those in Europe.

Looking at the history of international law as a history of an encounter between Europe and non-European peoples, means viewing European expansion and imposition of European law as violent and disruptive, not peaceful and law oriented, as for most peoples in the world European contact also resulted in a loss (to varying degrees) of independence. This was the antithesis of the narrative of progress; in fact, it has been an erasure. So, from this point of view it is the messy encounter between Europe and other peoples that has been central to how the doctrine of unilateral acts has developed (Anghie 2006; see generally Benton 2002).

As a result, any history of international law is inherently problematic as it is based on the European concept of sovereignty that has been foundational to international law (Yasuaki 2000). This book acknowledges this problem and endeavours to highlight this relationship. However, it ultimately adopts the conventional historical periods most often used in international law—the "pre-modern," that is prior to the Peace of Westphalia in 1648, the "traditional," or classical, which lasted from approximately 1648–1900, and the modern, which has lasted from the World War I on (D. Kennedy 1988–1989, 13). This periodization will be used because the doctrine of unilateral acts is a product of the post-1648 structure of international law, although this is done knowing the limits and violence of this approach for non-European peoples.

The aim of this work is to trace the history of the legal understanding of unilateral acts, from the classical period of international law onwards, in order to see how they have been understood, formalized, and implemented in legal practice. The classical period is chosen as a starting point because in the nineteenth century (European) states commonly accepted that unilateral acts were legally binding only when a formal treaty secured their obligations (*The Law Review of British and Foreign Jurisprudence* 1849, 266). Consequently, the majority of acts that we now understand as unilateral acts were not considered "legal acts"; they were considered "political" or "diplomatic" acts that had no legal effect unless they were also formalized into a treaty. However, there were two key areas where unilateral acts were considered to have independent legal implications: declarations of independence and unilateral declarations ending wars. This book will trace how the doctrine has expanded outward from these two examples of binding unilateral acts to become the category of legal obligation held today.

Unilateral Acts in the Nineteenth Century

Before turning to unilateral acts in the nineteenth century, such as declarations of independence and declarations ending wars, it is important to outline, briefly, the state of international law at this time. Bowden has argued

> The various civilizations and empires that dominated corners of Europe at different times all resorted to violent conquest to further their cause and expand their dominion. So too, for centuries Europe's violence and exploitation was directed inward toward conquering immediate neighbouring peoples just as much as it was directed at distant peoples. It was not until the seventeenth and eighteenth centuries that European cleavages began to ameliorate, slowly being replaced by a modicum of cohesion and solidarity, at least among (Western) European nations.
>
> (Bowden 2005, 3)

Therefore, Europe's expansionist tendencies may be traced to the "First Crusade" or as Bowden does to 1245 when Pope Innocent writes his "decretal" *Quod Super His* on "papal-infidel relations" (Bowden 2005, 4). This declaration had a profound impact on the first group of scholars who would wrestle with the "discovery" of the "New World." These scholars, often called the Spanish "scholastic" scholars, wrote in the sixteenth and into the early seventeenth centuries about the debates over the status and rights of those peoples already living in North or South America (Bowden 2005, 8).

This history then is generally traced through the work of major scholars such as Grotius, Puffendorf, Vatel, Wolf, Bynkershoek, and eventually in the late nineteenth century, Wheaton (Bowden 2005, 13; Koskenniemi 2002, 2). Further, their work is often tied to major "beginnings" for international law, such as noted previously, the Peace of Westphalia or sometimes the Congress of Vienna (Koskenniemi 2002, 2).

In contrast to these histories, Koskenniemi argues, there was a fundamental shift in what he terms the "sensibility" of international law over the course of the nineteenth century, with a fundamental break in thinking around 1870 (Koskenniemi 2002, 3–4). Therefore, if the names cited previously or dates mentioned seem abstract, the broad point here is that although acts, such as unilateral acts, can be situated within the broad sweep of the history of international law, a strong argument can be made that something fundamental changed over the nineteenth century. Koskenniemi argues that this is an emergence of "a new professional self-awareness" around international law (Koskenniemi 2002, 4) that this work argues marks the shift towards legalization of these acts. So, while the existence of antecedent acts in international law cannot be denied, the starting point to study the doctrine of the history of unilateral acts can be situated in the changes in the doctrine that took place over the nineteenth century. Further, as Koskenniemi, Anghie, Bowden, and others note, this shift cannot be meaningfully separated from the fact that as Koskenniemi says, summarizing a contemporary writer,

> Europeans still acted from a position of superiority over others: Capitulation regimes, consular jurisdiction, brutal colonial wars had become banal aspects of the international every day. Advancing civilization [in the European view] oppressed and impoverished indigenous populations to the point of extinction—a fact accepted by imperial powers as an inevitable consequence of modernity.
>
> (Koskenniemi 2002, 98)

Concepts that organized international law at this time, such as the "standard of civilization," emerged out of European theories of natural law and were therefore dependent on cultural context. This meant that all peoples did not need to be treated equally but could be judged against Europe for their "standard of civilization" (Bowden 2005, 15–16; Koskenniemi 2002, 100). This shift came about with the loss of the influence of religion and rise of nation states in the preceding centuries, in short, the secularization of international law, to the point that these ideas came to be treated as an inevitable part of international law (Bowden 2005, 17). So, at the start of the nineteenth century indigenous populations remained unable to meet the standard of civilization and therefore could not participate in international law (and by extension could be colonized) (Koskenniemi 2002, 115). Individuals could hold natural rights, but not peoples or communities. These tensions created debate over the scope and limits to colonizing such peoples, and this was a moving target based on "what Europeans approved" (Koskenniemi 2002, 129, 135). This tension between colonizing and legalizing impulses continued into the twentieth century but arguably emerged most forcefully and shifted over the nineteenth century up to the end of World War I when it became associated with the next shaping force to guide international legal thinking, liberal internationalism (Koskenniemi 2002, 176).

I argue that these broad shifts can be seen in the ways that unilateral acts were viewed over the course of the century and are also tied to the "grand redeeming project" (Bowden 2005) of international law that has emerged in the form of legalization. Legalization, arguably, is the flipside of what Koskienniemi has called the link between "progress and civilization" that sustains international law. This is because legalization is a technique to administer international law, and administration has been key to the ways international law has operated ever since it had to encounter non-European peoples. (See for example, (Koskenniemi 2002, 176.) In the nineteenth century, legalization emerged as a key force in shaping the colonial encounter. However, as stated, in regard of unilateral acts, these acts were generally considered to be political acts unless they were codified into the form of a binding agreement between recognized states, a treaty.

The Paris Declaration on Maritime Law of 1856 exemplified a declaration that was distilled into written treaty form. In his treatise on international law, the 1910 edition, Westlake noted that this declaration was legally authoritative because it was signed by all the relevant parties or they had received the instructions of their Court to participate in the Declaration. Similarly, he noted that the St. Petersburg Declaration of 11 December 1868, which prohibited the use of explosive bullets of a weight of less than 400 grammes had not been ratified when it was declared. He used these examples to argue that ratification was not a requirement for these declarations to become legally binding because they represented the assent of the "highest contracting authorities of the state," but if a declaration was issued without this authority then Westlake presumed that ratification by the sovereign was required (Westlake, *International Law* 1910, 293). This is important because it illustrates Westlake's attempts to rationalize unilateral declarations within treaty formalities.

In making this statement Westlake conceptualized a declaration as a form of a treaty. In his view, a declaration was legally binding when it took the form of a written declaration backed up by consent of the highest authorities of the state through their signature. So, by reverse inference, if this was his requirement for a legally binding declaration then any unwritten declarations or acts were not legally binding and were purely political. Moreover, it was important to note that only plenipotentiaries of recognized states were capable of entering into such binding declarations. Again by inference, an entity that was not a state (and this was most of the world since this was the height of colonial expansion) was automatically excluded from making a binding unilateral act.

A second form of unilateral act that was common in the nineteenth century was the declaration of independence. Interestingly, declarations of independence raised the possibility of an entity transitioning from a non-sovereign entity to an independent state. This was important because it illustrated the challenges in the encounters between European colonial powers and non-European peoples. It is also still current. For example, the issue of the validity of declarations of independence has re-emerged in the twenty-first century in, for example, the case of Kosovo, which is the subject of Chapter 6. In the nineteenth century, the main site of unilateral declarations of independence was Central and South America. One example of a nineteenth-century declaration of independence took place in Argentina, which proclaimed its independence from Spain in 1816.

Argentinian independence was declared at a "General Congress" of representatives of various peoples in the United Provinces, as Argentina was then called. There they voted to declare themselves independent from King Ferdinand VII of Spain, and granted themselves the "high character of a nation."[1] But, under nineteenth-century international law, it was only when other states recognized the declaration that it had legal impact. This issue of recognition was key, as admission to the community of states was explicitly a matter of judgment by the (very limited, predominantly Euro-American) community of states. So, even though unilateral acts were theoretically permitted by international law, in the nineteenth century it was only when other states recognized this declaration that it became valid. The issue of recognition of unilateral acts is an important one, and it will receive sustained discussion in Chapter 3 when the issue of autonomy of unilateral acts is considered, and it is an important element of Chapter 4, which focuses on the relationship between unilateral acts and estoppels.

Recognition was at issue in the case of *United States v. Hutchings*, where the US Supreme Court was asked to consider the independence of Argentina, and whether or not it had achieved sovereignty by 1816. According to Chief Justice Marshall, Argentina was not legally independent until the executive of a state (i.e. the United States) recognized the new nation. In another case, in 1818, Marshall clarified that it was the body with the power over foreign relations that had the authority to recognize a new state. Politically, in case of claims of independence from Spain, the United States had adopted an official policy of neutrality and so did not recognize claims of independence by states controlled by Spain, such as Argentina. This policy of neutrality (although officially in effect after 1818) came to a head in 1816 with Argentina's formal declaration of independence. This declaration led President Monroe to seek advice from his cabinet on whether or not he had power to recognize the new state. Cabinet demurred on this question until 1819 at which time Secretary

1 The full text of the declaration can be found in (Mills, Taylor, & Lauderdale Graham 2002, 401–402).

of State Adams prepared instructions that recognition could not take place until the territory in possession of the new state matched the scope of its declaration. Recognition was then further delayed by negotiations between Spain and the United States over Florida, and occurred only in 1822 once those were completed as part of the famous "Monroe Doctrine" which will be discussed in detail in the next chapter (Robertson 1918, 239–240, 243–252).

This example illustrates that in the early nineteenth century declarations of independence did not have legal authority, but the "facts" that the declaration represented, effective control, and independence, did. And there was a clear hierarchy of states that were capable of both giving and receiving such recognition.

Westlake reflected on this hierarchy of states in the early twentieth century when he explained that, legally, colonies were not in "real union" with the home state, because they were unequal. As such, the position of colonies was one of dominion where their external sovereignty was held by the "parent state" (Westlake, *International Law* 1910, 40–41). They were not sovereign or independent. Importantly, he wrote, without any reflection, that

> [t]he international society which develops international law by its controlling opinion, enforces it by its irregular opinion, and receives or claims to receive its full application to all its members, is composed of all the states of European blood, that is of all the European and American states, except Turkey and of Japan. Outside Europe there were three Christian states to the dealings which international law would be considered to apply, though they can hardly be ranked as contributing to its development or enforcement—Abyssinia, backward in civilization, the little republic of Liberia, and the late Congo state, which might have been reckoned as Christian in respect of its sovereign being the King of the Belgians, though its population was African and Heathen.
>
> (Westlake, *International Law* 1910, 40)

He continued, "Beyond the above limits the international society exercises the right of admitting states to parts of its law without admitting them to the whole of it" (Westlake, *International Law* 1910, 40). So, Westlake clearly believed that not all peoples could declare independence unilaterally as for most states they had status as a Dominion. As a result, independence required the consent of the colonial government and to gain this consent the state must be Christian or be accepted by existing states as civilized. This was not, and was not intended to be, an equally applied form of a unilateral act.

Additionally, declarations were traditionally one way to end wars. As Wright noted in his survey of the termination of wars between 1480 and 1970, most did not end by peace treaty and none ended by treaty after World War I. He specifically noted that in the nineteenth century peace could be achieved unilaterally either temporarily, through 'suspension of arms' or ceasefire, or more permanently by armistice or truce. However, military commanders could also unilaterally end the conflict without the permission of their government (although this could be repudiated, as it was by the British at El Arish) through capitulation or surrender. Lastly, he noted that peace could be made without unconditional surrender through a unilateral declaration of the victor (Wright 1970, 52, 55–56). In fact, Westlake held that hostilities should generally be concluded by treaty, implying that up to the twentieth century any of these other ways of ending hostilities were political or a matter of diplomatic practice and honour unless a treaty was also concluded (Westlake, *International Law* 1910, 5).

In sum, two themes emerge from the nineteenth-century approaches to unilateral acts. First, unilateral declarations were not considered a separate category of legal obligation, as these acts were not "legal" unless they were subsequently affirmed in a treaty, and to sign a treaty an entity had to be a state. Second, it was the existing state that had the power to determine when an entity could claim independence. The nature of international society in the nineteenth century meant that only sovereign, equal, European states were capable of turning their declarations into treaties. An extreme example of this was the General Act of the Conference of Berlin, 1885, in which representatives of major European powers, Prussia, Austria, France, the United Kingdom, Belgium, Denmark, Italy, Netherlands, Sweden-Norway, Portugal, and Spain, and powers such as Russia, the United States, and the Ottoman Empire jointly declared, in a treaty format, the future of West Africa (South African History Online n.d.). No African representatives were present and the conference has been interpreted as "canonical" in European colonization in the continent (although its meaning and impact are discussed widely, see generally, Craven (2015)). Further, as is evident from this example, only states that met the definition of "civilized" were capable of declaring independence, and then only with the permission of an existing state. In short, in the nineteenth century, unilateral acts were applied narrowly, as a form of a promise between sovereign states, or as part of the way of recognizing a new state but they were not a separate category of "law".

In the rest of this book I will trace the struggle to "legalize" the category of unilateral acts from its nineteenth-century foundations into a broad category of obligation. To understand why and how this occurred, this book will examine the history of the legal doctrine of unilateral acts. This history will show that in spite of efforts to progressively make unilateral acts "legal," they still have not been precisely defined or easy to apply, problems that challenge the very commitment these acts are meant to establish. This history will illustrate both the processes and challenges of "legalization". And, as a result, I will argue that legalization of these acts is only partial so that there are major hurdles still to overcome. Consequently, it is more important to discuss individual forms of unilateral acts (such as promises, notifications, or reservations) as obligations in international law while acknowledging that, as a category, unilateral acts are best understood as acts that contribute to the creation of international laws. This argument, in itself, is not novel. There have been critics of unilateral acts as a source of legal obligation (see for example (A.P. Rubin 1977), but what is new here is the systematic historical tracing of this critique and the framing of this history as part of the process of legalization.

The Aims and Structure of This Book

There has not been, to my knowledge, any work that focuses specifically on the history and development of the doctrine of unilateral acts. By taking this approach I provide a fresh perspective on unilateral acts and how they have changed over time, to the debates within international law about what unilateral acts are and how they work, and to broader discussions about how international law is created.

Methodologically, this book is firmly situated in historiography. As Berg notes, however, historiography is not just an examination of past events, it also requires theoretical explanation of these events (Berg 2009, 296). Theory, on the other hand is the best "logical" explanation of these problems (Berg 2009, 23). Thus, this book uses the tools of historiography, and as will be seen later, critical legal history, to examine the past and reach the best explanation it can of this problem. Theoretically, this book proposes that the concept of legalization best explains the conceptual and definitional challenges that unilateral acts have presented for the doctrine of international law.

To be more specific, this book uses the methods of critical legal history, which as Gordon explains is an attempt to "rewrite" the history of legal doctrine (R. Gordon 1984, 57) in order to raise critiques of the legal "status quo" (R. Gordon 1984, 57). Doctrine is, essentially, a prescriptive or normative form of discourse (E. Rubin 1998, 1847 ff). And as such, this book engages in a history of a discourse. As Gordon notes, the "impulse" of historians who have adopted a discursive approach to history has been to highlight the indeterminate nature and social construction (Gordon 1984) of the ideas they studied. This is not to imply that these acts are divorced from their material reality, their existence in the world. However, they are interested in how the history of the discourse in question, in this case of unilateral acts, has been affected by this reality. This is what Foucault calls the effect of "putting-into-discourse" (Foucault 1990). This type of thinking has been called "historical epistemology" because its point is not to define how discourses have shaped real practices in the world, although those practices are real and have meaning that has been shaped by the discourse, but to trace the continuities and breaks in that discourse itself (P. Gordon n.d.).[2] To put it plainly, this book will examine how the doctrine of unilateral acts has changed over time by examining the key events and cases that have shaped these ideas.

To do this, the following chapters will outline the doctrine of unilateral acts from their nineteenth-century origins up to the twenty-first century. I have

2 See reference to Arnold Davidson in Gordon.

adopted a chronological approach not only for historical clarity but because this chronology also overlaps with the main developments in the "legalization" of unilateral acts. As noted earlier, I propose that the best explanation of the complicated history of unilateral acts is legalization, as outlined by Abbot et al,., previously as the attempt to "institutionalize" legal acts (Abbott, et al. 2000). Legalization provides a way to make sense of the repeated, different attempts to incorporate unilateral acts into the doctrine of international law and why each of these attempts have faced challenges. It is these steps to legalization that provide the main focus of each chapter and the natural break points between chapters. This chronological approach does not, however, view legalization as a linear process. It first traces the attempts to establish unilateral acts as a category, but then the doctrine circles back as it tries to clarify this doctrine and implement it in practice.

Chapter 2 begins from the premise that up to the nineteenth century international legal discourse treated unilateral acts as diplomatic or political acts. This chapter then goes on to examine how, over the course of the nineteenth century, international law began to grapple with these acts in a meaningful way; by the end of the century these acts were, at times, considered to be binding through a state's tacit or actual consent.

The first attempt to legalize these acts, as consent-based obligations, eventually gave way to the interpretation of these acts as obligations *erga omnes*, the subject of Chapter 3. The formal categorization of unilateral acts as legal acts then led to attempts to make these acts more "precise." As a result, the doctrine then turned to the relationship between unilateral acts and estoppels, the topic of Chapter 4. These doctrinal developments, which are found mostly in the case law at the International Court of Justice (ICJ), impact heavily on the International Law Commission's attempt to codify this area of law, which is discussed in Chapter 5. In Chapter 6 this history of legalization has been traced up to the second decade of the twenty-first century with the International Court of Justice's Advisory Opinion on Kosovo, *Accordance With International Law of the Unilateral Declaration of Independence in Respect of Kosovo.*

To sketch this history each chapter uses case studies of key unilateral acts or key legal decisions or attempts to codify unilateral acts in order to highlight the state of legalization at that time. Case studies, as a method of research, are the "gathering of enough information about a particular person, social setting, event, or group to permit the researcher to effectively understand how the subject operates or functions" (Berg 2009, 317). It is designed to take doctrinal debates and place them in what Yin has called "real world context" (Yin 2011, 16n). This method is particularly effective for studying the legalization of unilateral acts given the fact that that they have not been clearly defined and they encompass such a wide range of acts that covering them all comprehensively would be beyond the scope of this (or any one) book. Thus, the purpose of this research is to choose cases that are illustrative of the general approach to unilateral acts taken in the period in question and use that as a descriptive "snapshot" for the time (Berg 2009, 293). Further, because of the leading nature of these cases, they have had outsized effect on the understanding of the doctrine of unilateral acts, which means their approaches can lead to some predictive statements about their role and impact on legalization of unilateral acts (Berg 2009, 295–296).

Specifically, Chapter 2 begins to explore the doctrine of unilateral acts in "modern" international law, a process that, as noted earlier, has its roots in the nineteenth century. In this time period, unilateral acts came to be seen as a product of tacit consent. However, unilateral acts in this time period were also sometimes considered political or diplomatic acts and were not always evaluated legally. A primary example of this second trend is the Monroe Doctrine of 1823. The Monroe Doctrine was a statement of the US President with clear international implications. But this chapter will show that contemporaneous and even later interpretations of the act did not always consider it a legal act. Chapter 2 uses the Monroe Doctrine as illustrative of the approach to unilateral acts in the nineteenth century. This example also describes the process by which a unilateral act was "legalized" as well as the limits to this approach.

This chapter will also show how, over the course of the twentieth century, the doctrine around unilateral acts took on an increasingly legal tone. This point will be illustrated by the legal advice given to President Kennedy during the Cuban Missile Crisis that the Monroe Doctrine was a regional custom. These developments reached their high point in the mid-1970s with the decisions of the International Court of Justice collectively (and commonly) called the *Nuclear Tests Cases.* These cases revolved around Australia and New Zealand's challenge to the legality of France's above-ground nuclear testing in the South Pacific. The Court dodged this question by deciding that French public statements that they would stop above-ground tests created a legally binding obligation that was both unilateral and binding *erga omnes* (as a promise made to the world at large). This decision expanded the scope of unilateral acts to include obligations that could arise without a specific addressee (i.e. another named state) for that promise (i.e. not an informal agreement).

Thus, Chapter 3 focuses on the *Nuclear Tests Cases* as the bedrock of the premise that unilateral acts created obligations *erga omnes.* However, much like the previous chapter, Chapter 3 notes how difficult it has been to apply these legal principles in practice. Particularly, this chapter illustrates how challenging it has been to separate legal from non-legal acts when theorizing unilateral acts as *obligations erga omnes.*

While the International Court of Justice has made broad statements about unilateral acts as obligations *erga omnes*, Chapter 3 also finds that they did not outline set procedures to determine when a unilateral act had this type of binding legal affect. As a result, there has been confusion between decisions on estoppel, a doctrine that allowed states to rely on the fact that other actors could not be both "hot and cold" on an issue, and decisions on unilateral acts.

Chapter 4 examines the case law of the International Court of Justice on estoppel both before and after the *Nuclear Tests Cases.* In this chapter, particular attention is given to the decision in the *Temple of Preah Vihear*, a case concerning sovereignty over a temple mount on the border between Cambodia and Thailand, which has been considered the quintessential case of estoppel at the International Court of Justice. This case will be particularly interesting because although it was decided in the 1960s, this dispute has been ongoing and it re-emerged at the Court in the twenty-first century.

Chapter 4 concentrates on the difficulties the Court has faced in separating unilateral acts that create legal obligations from acts of estoppel. This chapter suggests that the legalization of unilateral acts has not been fully realized. In particular, this chapter will argue that treating unilateral acts as acts of estoppel has not made it easier to determine which unilateral acts have international legal implications and which are non-legal, political, or diplomatic acts.

Next, Chapter 5 examines the work of the ILC on the topic of unilateral acts of states. The ILC worked on this topic for nearly 10 years, from 1996 to 2006, and this chapter will argue that in spite of all this hard work, the ILC's attempt at codification was not an advance on previous attempts to "legalize" unilateral acts. In the end, the ILC produced non-binding guidelines for states, which arguably did not solve the problems with the doctrine that were raised in earlier chapters. To build this argument, Chapter 5 focuses on several concepts that are core to the ILC's analysis—intention/will to create legal obligations, revocability, and estoppel. This chapter will show that the ILC was, until very recently, and without much success, still trying to work through how to understand and apply the doctrine of unilateral acts.

One result of the discussion in Chapters 2 through 5 is to identify the challenges that international law has faced in determining the scope of the category of unilateral acts. Chapter 6 picks up on this point, introducing the recent advisory opinion of the International Court of Justice, *Accordance with International Law of the Unilateral Declaration of Independence in Respect of Kosovo* in order to shine a light on the continued confusion between unilateral acts with legal implications and political acts. This chapter takes us full circle to a basic question: Without a definition, when does a unilateral act have legal (as opposed to political) affect? If this question cannot be answered, it is tough to see how one can argue that unilateral acts have been effectively legalized.

To begin to build this argument, the next chapter will examine the progressive legalization of unilateral acts from the mid-nineteenth century into the mid-twentieth century.

2 Unilateral Acts as Consent-Based Agreements

As the Introduction demonstrated, by the nineteenth century states accepted that unilateral acts could create the same rights and obligations indicated by a binding treaty (The Law Review of British and Foreign Jurisprudence 1849, 266). However, most of the acts that are now classified as unilateral acts were not considered "legal acts," they were considered "political" or "diplomatic" acts. And, in the cases when they were considered legal acts they were treated as discrete legal acts that did not have legal effect until they were codified in treaty form, or in the case of unilateral declarations of independence, the new state was recognized by other states. As the Introduction noted, the Monroe Doctrine was one key example of the progressive legalization of unilateral acts from the early nineteenth century onward.

In 1823, President Monroe included in his annual address a unilateral statement of the US policy in the Americas. In this declaration, he made three primary assertions. First, he reiterated the independence of all states in the Americas: "the American continents, by free and independent condition which they have assumed and maintained, are henceforth not to be considered as subjects for future colonization." Second, he warned European powers that, "we should consider any attempt on their part to extend their system to any portion of this hemisphere as dangerous to our peace and safety." Third, he asserted that the United States would take a position of neutrality in Europe's affairs (Monroe n.d., Gilderhus 2006, 8). This section of the address, which came to be called the Monroe Doctrine, has shaped US policy towards the Americas since its formulation (Gilderhus 2006, 6).

Importantly, the Monroe Doctrine was not originally perceived as a legal declaration. As Root noted in 1914, "[n]o one ever pretended that Mr. Monroe was declaring a rule of international law or that the doctrine which he declared has become international law" (Root 1914, 431). Similarly, in 1920 Tower argued that the doctrine was an American policy, not law (Tower 1920, 17). So, the Monroe Doctrine was not initially considered to have legal implications but this changed by the middle of the twentieth century. For example, in the 1960s, President Kennedy was given a legal opinion during the Cuban Missile Crisis that claimed that the Monroe Doctrine was a special law of the Western Hemisphere. As a result, it was argued, the Doctrine authorized unilateral military action by the United States. President Kennedy, however, rejected this advice (Chayes 1997).

What changed? The Monroe Doctrine's transition from a political act to a "special" regional custom, a binding legal obligation, was most likely linked to what Janis calls the "most exceptional aspect of American international law," its "belief long held by many Americans that the discipline embraces a utopian mission to substitute law and the courtroom for war and the battlefield" (Janis 2012, 533). This utopianism, which Janis traces to the early nineteenth century peace movement, was reinforced and exacerbated by a scarring civil war and so has a long history in American international law (Janis 2012, 533–544). However, it was World War I that Janis argues decisively changed American attitudes on international law, and turned sceptics such as President Woodrow Wilson (now a controversial president for his racism domestically) into proponents of world peace (Janis 2012, 544 ff). This utopianism was coincident with the expansion of the ambit of the doctrine of international law in Europe and in the United States (Vec 2012, 674). This tendency towards expanding the scope of international law can be seen in the European trend towards scientism that in turn led to the juridification of international law, and specifically a preference for codification in treaties. (See, generally, Vec (2012)). The European preference for treaty forms eventually combined with American utopianism when President Wilson's Fourteen Points were incorporated as the background for the Paris Peace Conference at the end of World War I. (See, generally, Kruger (2012, 680–681)).

One of the most important institutional developments to come out of the Paris Peace Conference was the League of Nations, which was established in Part I of the post-World War I Peace Treaties signed with each of the former belligerents (Kruger 2012, 684). Ideally established to maintain collective security, it is likely better known for its institution of "mandates" in former German colonies and in the territories of the vanquished Ottoman Empire (Kruger 2012, 685). While the League of Nations operated until 1946, its institutional legacy was the creation of several bodies that survived it such as the Permanent Court of International Justice, the predecessor to the International Court of Justice (Kruger 2012). Ironically, the United States never signed on to the League. Emerging powers such as the newly established Union of Soviet Socialist Republics joined only for a brief time right before World War II, and Germany joined in 1926 and withdrew in 1933 (National Membership of the League of Nations n.d.) as Adolf Hitler consolidated his power. This withdrawal allowed Germany to flout the post-World War I peace treaties and form individual alliances with states that eventually became the Axis countries in World War II. Germany's increasing belligerence (for example the annexation of Austria and Sudetenland) came to a head in 1939 with its invasion of Poland and the formal start to this new, second, World War (Kruger 2012, 693–694). In a great irony, Hitler used the Monroe Doctrine to argue for its right to expansion and non-intervention in its sphere of influence by other powers (Kruger 2012, 694).

At the time, President Roosevelt argued for what Kruger calls the "connection and interplay between the constitutional order of a state and its foreign policy principles, . . ." in his famous State of the Union Address known as the Four Freedoms (freedom of speech, freedom of worship, freedom from want, and freedom from fear) (Kruger 2012, 694). In spite of the utopian trend of this speech (which was consistent with contemporary American approaches to international law), there was a distinct lack of consensus during the interwar years about the US role in international law that led them to be isolationist for the first part of the War (Roskin 1974, 567). However, this all decisively shifted with the Japanese attack on Pearl Harbor (Roskin 1974, 567).

However, as Roskin notes, this post-Pearl Harbor shift to interventionism remained part of American foreign policy long after World War II. As he put it, "[b]y that time almost all sections of the globe now 'mattered' to American security, particularly as a new hostile power—the Soviet Union seemed bent on territorial and ideological aggrandizement" (Roskin 1974, 569). He observes that by 1955 the United States was committed to the defence of 70-plus states (Roskin 1974, 569).

From the nineteenth to the mid-twentieth century, American foreign policy veered between its long-held utopian strain and its protectionist/non-interventionist strain. From Wilson's Fourteen Points, to Roosevelt's Four Freedoms (and ultimately to his wife's role in drafting the United Nations Charter), it seemed that utopianism or, more properly perhaps, idealism, would develop and prevail as the leading theory of international law in the United States, in spite of the tragedies of the early part of the twentieth century. Moreover, the United States emerged from these events as a global superpower.

Indeed, Kennedy notes that intellectually, it was in the period in between the two world wars that a distinctive American approach to international law formed. This approach was largely based on humanitarian impulses but took the form of European formalism—a strong type of scientific (also called positivist) approaches to international law (Kennedy 1988–1989, 3). In relation to unilateral acts this approach can be seen to extend the nineteenth-century view that unilateral acts were binding only when codified into treaties. It was this ideal, of an obligation in which consent was indicated through a signature on a document, that became the model of a binding legal obligation. However, in cases where consent was not easily put into writing, such as a custom or unilateral act, it could also be indicated by tacit consent.

Kennedy also argues that post-World War II international lawyers were different than their interwar colleagues. They were idealists about international law and institutions, but their idealism was tempered by a pragmatism, and thus adapted (domestic American) critiques of formalism for the international arena. So, these scholars brought their anti-formalism as well as a support for international institutions into their practices of international law (Kennedy 1988–1989, 3–4). Not surprisingly, the meaning of the Monroe Doctrine changed precisely in line with these historical shifts. Further, these historical trends ushered in formal attempts to legalize unilateral acts, as will be traced through the history of the Monroe Doctrine.

The Monroe Doctrine: A Doctrine of Non-Intervention by a Great Power

Near the end of the first volume of the 1910 edition of his work on international law, Westlake mentioned the Monroe Doctrine. There he noted:

> The Monroe Doctrine proclaimed by the United States has often been cited as a parallel to the position asserted for themselves by the great powers for themselves by the Great Powers of Europe, and the two are indeed alike in being claims to regulate, more or less, the affairs of a quarter of the globe. But their relations to international law are different. The Monroe doctrine has not been systematically carried out by enforcing on the other American states arrangements in which they were not consulted, and there are signs that those states would not allow it to be so carried out. Consequently, it must stand, at least for the present, as a policy which the United States are entitled to entertain so far as its application may in each instance be justice, precisely as Great Britain and Russia have their policies for Central Asia; and it would be beside the scope of the present volume to examine its origin and development.
>
> (Westlake, International Law 1910, 324)

On first reading, Westlake's position is confusing, reflecting the ambiguous status of the doctrine itself. Was the Monroe Doctrine law or policy? And what were the entitlements of the countries of the Hemisphere that resisted this doctrine, or at the very least had an ambiguous relationship to it?

Westlake's comments on the Monroe Doctrine only make sense in the context of his understanding of the Great Powers of Europe—his yardstick for assessing the meaning of the Monroe Doctrine. In this regard, he noted that states had the rights of independence and equality, while then contradicting himself and arguing that the Great Powers were a "separate and recognized class". He adopted the interpretation of Lord Salisbury that the Great Powers were able to take "Federated action" in Europe, which Westlake predicted would lead to a government of states. But his vision of world government was not utopian—as he noted:

> [t]he world in which the largest intercourse of civilized men has been from time to time carried on has not always been distributed into equal and independent states, and we are reminded by what we see that it may not always continue to be so distributed.
>
> (Westlake, *International Law* 1910, 321–322, 323)

As a result of his positive assessment of Great Power relations, Westlake argued that as part of its sovereign powers a state could voluntarily agree to anything "stopping short of reducing itself to a condition of semi-sovereignty" (Westlake, *International Law* 1910, 323). Westlake was a paragon of British international law at the height of Empire and he could not conceive of the fact that some states may have seen sovereignty as their only barrier against aggressive interference by the Great Powers who had outsized influence on these smaller states.

Consequently, examining Westlake's analysis of the Monroe Doctrine in the context of his discourse on sovereignty raises two important points: First, Westlake interpreted the Monroe Doctrine as a unilateral statement of a "Great Power" to control a hemisphere. Second, Great Powers, whether the United States or a European power, could only apply these unilateral statements if smaller states apparently willingly agreed to this, even if it meant giving up their sovereignty.

Westlake's analysis navigated two tensions: The first tension was whether the Monroe Doctrine was a doctrine of non-interference. Did it allow a "Great Power" to intervene in the affairs of the hemisphere as it deemed appropriate? This tension became more evident as the United States became increasingly powerful. This led to a second tension: whether this doctrine had any legal effect or was only a political statement. These two tensions can be examined through the work of scholars active the time.

In 1881 Kasson noted that Calvo, an eminent Argentinian diplomat and scholar of international law, had focused his assessment of the Monroe Doctrine on the relationship between the doctrine and non-interference (Encyclopedia Britannica 2013). Calvo argued that all the nations of the Americas were civilized and independent, and they had no sovereign over them, making them equal to the Europeans powers. For Calvo, the Monroe Doctrine was premised on a policy of non-interference other than in the case of a legitimate war or where the interference permitted by a treaty (Kasson 1881, 523,525). In other words, for Calvo, the doctrine was not a statement that could be legally acted upon but it was a statement of a fact—colonial interference was prohibited in the Americas because they were part of the "civilized" nations of the world. However, at the end of the nineteenth century Moore argued that when the doctrine was promulgated this was not factually true. His assessment was that in 1823 "subjects of civilized powers" had not settled the entire continent (Moore 1896, 6). Moore's position can be seen as representative of a view that the states of the Americas still required intervention or tutelage.

Factually, the effectiveness of the Monroe Doctrine in this period was questionable. As Alvarez observed, sometimes Great Powers and the United States did pursue armed intervention without regard for the doctrine. However, as the power of the United States grew—as early as 1909 Alvarez described it as a hegemon—it not only enforced the Monroe Doctrine but actively expanded its scope to both prevent other states from interfering in affairs of the hemisphere or intervening in disputes in the hemisphere (Alvarez 1909, 298,

314–317). So, by the early twentieth century the United States was powerful enough to assert its policy of "non-intervention," by force if necessary. Or as Hull colourfully put it in 1914, "Jefferson's and Monroe's confidence in democracy has grown into a determination that our neighbors in the Western World shall enjoy for themselves, *nolens volens*, the blessings of constitutional government, even if we are obliged to blow these blessings upon them from the guns of superdreadnoughts" (Hull 1914, 159).

As a result, it seems fair to conclude, as Inman did in 1921, that the Monroe Doctrine was originally intended to exclude colonial powers from America and it was not meant to foster American intervention in South America. However, he noted that, over time

> the Monroe Doctrine has been a continual source of irritation to Hispanic American nations. At first they accepted it gladly, as we have seen, as protecting them from Europe, but later we see it becoming in their eyes an instrument through which the United States presumed to dictate to them. (Inman 1921, 649)

He explained that the doctrine became confused with three ideas, American leadership, imperialism, and Pan-Americanism, that were not part of the doctrine (Inman 1921, 648, 656–657). In fact, this became such a sore point that Secretary of State Hughes, on the centenary of the Monroe Doctrine, sought to publicly reassure that this confusion was not accurate and that it was a policy of non-intervention. These assurances were continually issued as late as 1930 (More Talk About the Monroe Doctrine 1930, 153). However, it is worth noting that these public statements were necessary because the actions of the United States belied their assertions. As Barratt noted, America had not been "faultless" in its international relations, as there had at times been a blatant disregard of sovereignty in the Americas, which led these states to fear the doctrine and dismiss it outright (Barrett 1928, 26).

The Monroe Doctrine: From Political Act to Special Law

These developments in the Monroe Doctrine meant that in the early twentieth century, the legal significance of Monroe's statement was widely debated. For example, in 1907 Simmons suggested that:

> When it was promulgated in 1824 it was purely a doctrine, adopted by the executive of the United States alone, and promulgated to the country and the world through a message of the chief executive, a doctrine intended to state a principle to guide the action of this country in the circumstances surrounding this continent. It became a policy, a step higher in importance, when the legislative joined the executive branch of the government in recognizing, by sending commissioners thereto, the

> purpose of the Panama Congress. That the United States never actually acted in that Congress and that Congress took no action involving the Doctrine except to adopt it as one of the matters to be considered, is of no importance. Thus, having become the policy of the government it so remained and remains unless and until some equally decisive government action repeals the policy. A policy adhered to and practiced by this government and recognized by all civilized governments, rises still further in the scale of importance, becomes an integral part of international law when it becomes a rule of conduct accepted as binding by all civilized states.
>
> (Simmons 1907, 244–245)

He further noted that The Hague Convention of 1899 included a provision reaffirming the US traditional policy of non-interference and by doing so Senate approval of the convention was secured (Simmons 1907, 246).

So, by the early twentieth century the contours of the mid-century debate over the legality of the doctrine were becoming clear—was it a national policy or an international doctrine? And, importantly for present purposes, if it was an international doctrine was it a custom of international law? The argument for interpreting the Monroe Doctrine as custom was based the fact that it was incorporated into treaties such as Article 21 of the Covenant of the League of Nations (The Covenant of the League of Nations n.d.). But this argument was countered by the fact that these provisions were included in these treaties in order to secure American participation.

To be able to start answering these questions, it is important to note how the United States perceived this doctrine as well as how it was received internationally. Influential Americans of this period such as Elihu Root, Secretary of State, asserted that the doctrine was not one of international law, per se, but it was an expression of the inherent right of self-defence. President William H. Taft and Secretary of State Hughes also made this point[1] (Sheppard 1924, 37; Inman 1921, 644–645; Barrett 1928, 4, 9–10,20–21). As Shepherd wrote the "connecting idea and purpose of the doctrine" was the "defense of the United States against aggression from overseas" (Sheppard 1924, 39).

However, when Shepherd tried to defend the doctrine, he was forced to concede that any time the Monroe Doctrine had been enforced it was not in self-defence. On this basis, he concluded that it was a unilateral policy of the United States but it did not reflect a regional understanding, implying that it was not a customary law of the region. On the other hand, some South American representatives, such as the Brazilian representative to the Permanent Court of Arbitration, Bevilaqua, argued that it was a principle of international law on the grounds that it had been included in The Hague Convention, a multilateral treaty (Sheppard 1924, 39, 51, 66; Barrett 1928, 22).

1 See for example, E. Root, quoted in (Inman 1921, 643–644).

This decision was consistent with the League of Nations' approach to international relations in which the commitment to consent was used to buttress a commitment to existing treaty law and, in a roundabout way, justify the legalization of the category of unilateral acts. In fact, Article 21 of the Covenant of the League of Nations, already discussed previously, specifically preserved sovereignty when it noted, "Nothing in this Covenant shall be deemed to affect the validity of international agreements, such as treaties of arbitration or regional understandings such as the Monroe Doctrine, for securing the maintenance of peace" (The Covenant of the League of Nations n.d.).

It has already been mentioned that this provision was considered the price of American assent to the text of the Covenant. As Garner noted,

> When the first draft of the Covenant, containing no reference to the Monroe Doctrine, was published in the United States, President Wilson was given to understand, in terms which he could not mistake, that without some provision intended to safeguard the Monroe Doctrine the Covenant would probably not be acceptable to the Senate.
>
> (Garner, The Recrudescence of the Monroe Doctrine 1930, 233)

This pressure eventually led President Wilson to propose the Amendment that became Article 21 (Garner, The Recrudescence of the Monroe Doctrine 1930, 234).

Although most states of the Americas eventually gave in to including reference to the Monroe Doctrine in the Covenant of the League of Nations, as Garner observed, Central and South American states were initially reluctant to accept a treaty with an "elastic" standard that the United States could potentially use to justify a wide range of actions. For example, El Salvador, before ratifying, sought clarification of the doctrine. And, the ex-President of Honduras, Bonilla, protested against including the Monroe Doctrine in Article 21 of the Covenant on the grounds that the treaty never defined the scope of the doctrine so it could encompass any American act. Mexico insisted that it had never recognized the Monroe Doctrine and that including reference to the doctrine would establish American "tutelage" over Latin America. Lastly, in 1928 Costa Rica appealed to the Council of the League of Nations for a definition of the doctrine (Garner, The Recrudescence of the Monroe Doctrine 1930, 234–236). In sum, in the early twentieth century, states in the Americas were drawing links between the Monroe Doctrine and non-consensual actions by the United States and they were concerned about including the doctrine in the Covenant. As these states had complex colonial histories, it is hardly surprising that they expressed concerns about formalizing unilateral statements that they perceived as affecting their sovereignty.

Over time it became clear that the United States was not joining the League and as a consequence, certain American and European Members began to call for withdrawing this Article of the Covenant. At the same time the United States began to take further steps to assert their interpretation of the Monroe

Doctrine, primarily through reservations to treaties such as the Kellogg-Briand Pact that ensured their ability to go to war to preserve the Monroe Doctrine. Garner noted that legally these reservations only applied to war in self-defence, a point that he argued reaffirmed the interpretation that the declaration was primarily intended for self-preservation (Garner, The Recrudescence of the Monroe Doctrine 1930, 234–235, 239, 241).

Collectively, these analyses indicate that before World War II, the Monroe Doctrine was not considered by states to be legal, per se, but the seeds of a legal interpretation were taking root. In fact, the idea of legality was so well planted that by 1936 Spencer felt obligated to write:

> an attempt to prove that the Monroe Doctrine does not constitute in itself a principle of international law but rather a purely political policy would appear completely superfluous in view of the well- nigh universal acceptance of this opinion, nevertheless, the reasons that dictate this conclusion are themselves of the utmost importance in appreciating subsequently the position of the doctrine in positive law.
>
> (Spencer 1936, 400)

And on this basis, he produced several reasons why the doctrine was not legal: First, the United States could not deprive other states of their right to permit intervention. Second, the doctrine was only regional in scope, not international. Third, the Monroe Doctrine had only been given a unilateral interpretation, which, although tacitly accepted, did not make it law. Fourth, the doctrine contradicted the law of self-defence (which it purported to implement) because it explicitly forbade any outside tribunal from judging whether self-defence had been exercised legitimately. And finally, it did not have the universal assent required to create international law.

He then considered whether the incorporation of the doctrine into various treaties and reservations to treaties could transform the doctrine into international law. On both these counts he decided it could not. He argued, against prominent publicists of his day such as Keith and Fauchille, that incorporating the Monroe Doctrine into the Covenant of the League of Nations, a multilateral treaty, did not transform it into a principle of international (i.e. a customary) law. Analyzing the text of Article 21, he argued that the wording of the provision referred directly to "regional understandings," even though it did not have the acceptance of all American states. And while this could be understood in several senses, for Spencer it was key that there had been no tacit "meeting of the minds" on this doctrine and so it had no legal effect, even within the Covenant. However, he noted that Article 21 did seem to give precedence to the doctrine over the words of the Covenant—a position that he argued was antithetical to the Covenant itself (Spencer 1936, 401–402,405, 409–413).

So, while Spencer built a strong argument for the non-legal nature of the Covenant, he was setting himself up against a turning tide. As he more or less explicitly noted, major commentators in this time period asserted that the doctrine had become legal on the basis of its inclusion in multilateral treaties such as The Hague Convention and the Covenant of the League of Nations. It was the nature of a multilateral treaty itself that ensured that the doctrine could have force of law; the "universal" consent required for these treaties could have the effect of creating a custom. In any event, Spencer was already out of step with the doctrine of his times, and new attempts to institutionalize unilateral acts developed within the jurisprudence.

The doctrinal link between unilateral acts and consent was almost certainly tied to the ascendance of positivism in the discourse of nineteenth-century international law. As Pellet has explained and as well established in the literature,

> during the nineteenth century, international law scholars themselves were greatly influenced by the scientific philosophy of August Comte and others, and, trying to win the esteem which attached to pure scientists, they had a tendency to invent dogmas that were supposed to explain the law in the same way as mathematical postulates or physical "laws" explain mathematics or physics.
>
> (Pellet 1988–1989, 23)

From this scientific world view, legal positivism was "based on the simple assertion that the proper description of law is a worthy objective" and that description of the law was morally neutral and judgment free (Bix 2003, 33). However, one result of positivism's commitment to moral neutrality was that consent to legal obligations became (and arguably has remained) the cornerstone of international legal obligations.

The case that has often been cited as an example of positivism's pervasive influence, as well as the seminal statement of its consensual approach to international law, was the *SS Lotus Case*, a case before the Permanent Court of International Justice, (PCIJ) the interstate tribunal established by the League of Nations, rendered in 1927 (The Case of the SS Lotus 1927). This case came to the Court when Turkey sued France for damages over a collision at sea. In August 1926 a French mail ship, the Lotus, collided on the High Seas with a Turkish "collier," the Boz Kourt, cutting it in half and killing eight on the Turkish ship. The French ship saved those who could be saved and continued on to its final destination in Constantinople. On arrival, Turkish authorities investigated and proceeded to charge the officer on watch on the Lotus, Lieutenant Demons. They tried him for manslaughter, eventually sentencing him to 80 days in jail and a fine of 22 pounds (The Case of the SS Lotus 1927, 10, 11–12).

France argued that Turkish actions against its national, M. Demons, constituted a violation of international law, as all actions for breaches of "navigation regulations" fell only to the "flag state" under which the ship sailed—in this case France. As a result the Court defined the legal issue before it as question of permission. Was Turkey barred by international law from taking action against Lieutenant Demons under its own laws? (The Case of the SS Lotus 1927, 12,15).

In this case the Court famously noted that:

> [i]nternational law governs relations between independent States. The rules of law binding upon States therefore emanate from their own free will as expressed in conventions or by usages generally accepted as expressing principles of law and established in order to regulate the relations between these co-existing independent communities or with a view to achievement of common aims. Restrictions upon the independence of States cannot therefore be presumed.
>
> (The Case of the SS Lotus 1927, 18)

As a result, the Court then had to decide whether or not there existed a positive law, of treaty or custom, which prohibited states from exercising their criminal jurisdiction in cases such as the Lotus; it found none. This led the PCIJ to address the French government's second argument, that according to international law it, as flag state, had jurisdiction over the prosecution. And the Court found here too that there was no positive rule of treaty or custom prohibiting the flag state in which the effects of an act were felt from exercising jurisdiction over the act, since they, like France, were a flag state of a ship involved in the act. In fact, the Court indicated that customary practice seemed to show the opposite. The only question that remained was whether there was a special custom in relation to collision cases and again the Court could not find evidence of a custom. A split Court, with the President, the eminent Judge Huber, casting the deciding vote, held for Turkey (The Case of the SS Lotus 1927, 21–32).

Given these findings, scholars often state that the Lotus case established that anything not expressly prohibited by international law was permitted to states as part of states' rights as sovereign powers. The Court gave its support to this strong version of sovereignty and as Pellett has explained, it was a "classical voluntarist's analysis" in which "will would be the basis, the test, and the sign of the law at the same time" (Pellet 1988–1989, 26; Anghie 2005, 132).

In light of the *Lotus Case*, one early decision that was important for the development of the doctrine of unilateral acts was the *Eastern Greenland Case*, which was heard at the PCIJ as well. Scholars have often cited this decision as an example of a unilateral declaration.[2] The case, which was heard by the PCIJ in 1933, resulted from a dispute that emerged when Norway issued a

2 As Franck noted, prior to the *Nuclear Test Cases* decision, "[o]ne case stands out in the jurisprudence "—the *Eastern Greenland Case*. For an example of a scholar who examined the Eastern Greenland decision, see generally (Garner, The International Binding Force of Unilateral Oral Declarations, 1933; Franck 1975, 615).

proclamation claiming named territories in Eastern Greenland that Denmark argued was Danish territory. While there was a long history between the two countries, including union at one point, the issue really came to a head during World War I when Denmark ceded its territories in the West Indies. In doing so Denmark sought recognition of its interests in Greenland and permission to extend its activities there. The United States agreed to this, and, as the Islands were ceded in 1916, issued a statement that it would not object to Denmark extending its interests in Greenland. Then, at the end of World War I, the Danish Government was informed that there would be a Committee at the Peace Conference to deal with Claims to Spitzbergen, an Archipelago in the Greenland Sea. At this time, the Danish Government position was to raise no objection to this claim, but they notified Norway that they would be interested in raising their interests in Greenland before this Committee. To this the Norwegian Foreign Minister, Mr. Ihlen, first replied that they would "consider the question" but several days later he said "that the Norwegian Government would not make any difficulties in the settlement of this question" (Hudson n.d., 151–163).

As a result, the issue before the Court in this case was "whether the Ihlen declaration—even if not constituting a definitive recognition of Danish sovereignty—did not constitute an engagement obliging Norway to refrain from occupying any part of Greenland" (Hudson n.d., 190). The Court was concerned with the capacity of a statement made by a foreign minister to bind their government; its reasoning centred on the power of a diplomat make a binding declaration for his state in the course of ongoing negotiations (Hudson n.d., 151ff). The decision held that "The Court considers it beyond all dispute that a reply of this nature given by the Minister for Foreign Affairs on behalf of his Government in response to a request by the diplomatic representative of a foreign Power, in regard to a question falling within his province, is binding upon the country to which the Minister belongs" (Hudson n.d., 192).

The Court treated the declaration as a question of fact. The PCIJ asked whether a statement made by a Foreign Minister in international negotiations could be binding on the state that made the statement. However, it is questionable whether the case represents a unilateral act since Ihlen's statement was made in the context of ongoing negotiations and was part of an exchange, a *quid pro quo*. This focus on negotiations meant that the *Eastern Greenland Case* was really concerned with tacit consent. As Garner noted, when he analyzed this case,

> [t]he conclusion to the whole matter would seem to be that an oral agreement between states is, or may be, as binding upon the parties as if it were recorded in writing, and will be applied by international tribunals whenever the facts as to the agreement may be proved.
>
> (Garner, The International Binding Force of Unilateral Oral Declarations 1933, 497)

Garner argued that binding unilateral acts were a form of oral agreement based on tacit consent and he never mentioned unilateralism.

As a result, the opinion given to President Kennedy—that the Monroe Doctrine was a special law—expanded on the preference for consent outlined above, as well as relying on an approach that had emerged in the scholarly writing leading up to the end of World War II. By the 1950s opinions that unilateral acts could have independent legal effect had already been "floated" by scholars who tried to separate these acts from treaties (Fitzmaurice 1958; Schwarzenberger 1955). These scholars argued that it was necessary to have an enforceable category of unilateral obligations to maintain good faith in international relations. Two scholars in particular contributed to this argument, Schwarzenberger and Fitzmaurice.

Schwarzenberger and Fitzmaurice were proponents of the view that an international legal obligation arose from the intention of a state and the autonomy of the act. In a course he taught at The Hague Academy in 1955, Schwarzenberger asserted the legal character of unilateral acts. He argued that:

> If a subject of international law chooses to take up a position in relation to a matter, which is legally relevant and communicates this intent to others it is bound within such limits to accept the legal implications of such a unilateral act. If it acts contrary to its notified intent, it breaks the rule on the binding character of communicated unilateral acts.
>
> (Schwarzenberger 1955, 312)

He traced the legitimacy of this rule to the "obnoxiousness of contradictory behaviour" enshrined in the principle of *venire contra factum proprium*. He argued that this principle had assisted in the development of the rule of *opinio juris*, the need for the subjective belief in the legality of the act, in custom. From this basis, it had grown into a self-justifying rule of international law. He provided two examples of state practice to justify this contention, state recognition and wartime blockades.

For his example of recognition, Schwarzenberger referenced a note by the British Government to the Government of Persia (now Iran) that confirmed the independence of Afghanistan. This note affirmed earlier acts of the British Government recognizing Afghan sovereignty. As an example of wartime blockade, Schwarzenberger discussed British practice during the US Civil War. During the civil war, Britain asserted its right as a neutral state to sail into Confederate ports closed by Union ships. The British government argued that preventing their ships from entering these ports was a violation of their rights as a neutral state (Schwarzenberger 1955, 312–313).

Schwarzenberger's analysis had two problems. The first problem was the fact that he derived a separate category of unilateral acts from the principle of *contra factum*. Schwarzenberger offered no proof as to when or how the doctrine of *contra factum* became substantively separate from its role in creating *opinion juris*, that is, from the subjective belief in the legality of an act required for custom formation. He also did not clarify how this principle was distinct from estoppels, a reciprocal legal act which is the focus of Chapter 4, as he took his point as a matter of fact. The second problem was the appropriateness of his examples from state practice. Schwarzenberger's examples were both obscure and narrow. Britain's recognition of Afghanistan was actually an example of Britain's refusal to bow to Persian pressure to withdraw recognition of Afghanistan. It was not a new unilateral act; it was the continuation of an act of recognition, which had long been accepted as necessary to create a new sovereign state. (For a good analysis of all these arguments, see Rubin 1977.) As a result, this example did not prove Schwarzenberger's point, since it did not establish that states believed it was illegal, as opposed to politically expedient or diplomatic, to refuse to continue recognition of a state. And it was a stretch to argue that British practice during the US Civil War was a unilateral act. Schwarzenberger did not demonstrate that this act had independent legal effect from existing law. This example only confirmed that states could always exercise rights of neutrality they possessed under customary international law. If these were the most appropriate examples, then Schwarzenberger changed legal doctrine on thin precedent. In spite of these weaknesses Schwarzenberger confidently stated that unilateral acts had "legal effect." He based this obligation on the intention on the part of the state to be bound by their actions.

Similarly, a few years later—in the late 1950s—Fitzmaurice published a review and comment on the jurisprudence of the ICJ. In this review, he discussed the concept of unilateral declarations. He asserted that there were of three kinds of unilateral acts, "(i) [b]ilateral or multilateral Declarations which are unilateral neither in substance nor in form; (ii) . . . [those] that are unilateral both in form and substance; and (iii) . . . [those]that are unilateral in form but not in substance" (Fitzmaurice 1958, 229–230). He argued that unilateral acts in category (i) were tacit treaties and that as treaties these acts had legal effect according to the principles of treaty interpretation. He contended that acts in category (iii) were contractual and that declarations in this category were made in exchange for a "*quid pro quo*." These acts were not really unilateral; the exchange element made it similar to a contract, a form of treaty. In fact, these acts could also be interpreted according to principles of treaty interpretation. He cited the *Iranian Oil Case* as proof of this type of unilateral acts (Fitzmaurice 1958, 230–231). So, acts in categories (i) and (iii) were binding because of their reciprocity or exchange that led to a "*quid pro quo*".

It was Fitzmaurice's second category that became particularly important to the history of unilateral acts. This category dealt with the situation in which a declaration was unilateral in form and substance. These acts were unilateral because they did not involve any agreement or *quid pro quo* between the parties. These acts were legal if the state undertaking the act intended it to be legal and if this intention existed, the act was open to interpretation according to principles of treaty interpretation. Fitzmaurice provided no reference to doctrine or state practice to back up his definition of a unilateral act. In short, Fitzmaurice's second category of unilateral act, an act unilateral in form and substance, was novel and unsubstantiated (Fitzmaurice 1958, 230–231).[3] As a result Schwarzenberger and Fitzmaurice each proposed original criteria for binding unilateral acts that were later adopted by the ICJ. Schwarzenberger proposed that a unilateral act had legal effect when a state intended to be bound by its act. Fitzmaurice severed this type of act from a tacit treaty by asserting the unilateral nature or autonomy of the act.

Consequently, in the years before World War II, the legal status of the Monroe Doctrine was buttressed in part by the doctrine's inclusion in the Covenant of the League of Nations. This consensual, positive, legal obligation was treated as evidence of the fact that this unilateral declaration had become a regional custom. Yet, the reaction of countries of the Americas to this assertion shows that there was a real fear that the attempt to enforce the obligation contained in the doctrine was actually contrary to their sovereign interests and that the terms of the Monroe Doctrine had not been fully negotiated out as treaty practice dictated. There were concerns about basing a legal obligation on declarations in the absence of clear consent. It was these concerns about legalization through consent that led to the rethinking of the doctrine by Schwarzenberger and Fitzmaurice—two scholars whose work would find echoes in the *Nuclear Tests Cases* decision which is the focus of the next chapter.

Conclusion

From its statement in 1824 until the mid-twentieth century, there was a radical shift in the way the Monroe Doctrine was viewed. At first it was considered a mere policy doctrine—a doctrine with no legal effect. But, as US influence grew within the Americas, an argument emerged that the doctrine had some, as yet unclear, legal effect in ensuring European non-intervention in the sphere of US interest. American political expansion led to a sense of unease in the region and the feeling that US assertions of the doctrine were tied to its growing power.

In this changed political reality the meaning of the Monroe Doctrine was fluid, but it was based in particular on the idea that states could be only be bound by factual indications of their consent. This shift toward consent, a key part of the positivist view of international law, was most famously stated in the *Lotus* case.

3 Rubin has written,

> [i]t may be concluded that State practice prior to the Nuclear Tests cases reveals no consensus supporting a rule asserting an international obligation to be created by a unilateral declaration uttered publicly and with the intent to be bound, in the absence of additional factors such as a negotiating context, an affirmative reaction to other states, a tribunal to receive the declaration officially, or a supporting preexisting obligation (Rubin 1977, 7). See also Rubin (1977, 11).

This case stood for the proposition that states' sovereign prerogatives were limited only by their consensual obligations, a position which Pellet considered a "voluntarist's analysis" of law (Anghie 2005, 132; Pellet 1988–1989). A voluntarist approach to international law implied that unilateral acts could create obligations when there was factual evidence of the act, and when there was a consensual indication of the will to be bound. However, the Monroe Doctrine illustrated the problems with applying this approach since it did not originate in a treaty (as in the *Eastern Greenland Case*) nor did it clearly indicate a will to be bound.

In regard of the Monroe Doctrine, consent had to be constructed. This led to the strained argument that treaty texts signalled a commitment by states to consensually limit sovereignty and, in particular, indicated regional consent to the Monroe Doctrine, making it legally binding as a regional custom. This argument was most forcefully advanced regarding Article 21 of the League of Nations Covenant. But, to make this argument effective, the Monroe Doctrine had to meet the requirements of custom, consistent state practice followed by a belief that the doctrine was law.[4] These elements were difficult to demonstrate given the fact that during the period in question states in the region were not uniformly in favour of American assertions of non-intervention on their behalf. In fact, it seemed the more these assertions were made, while coinciding with the United States' growing power, the less there was consistent support expressed. Even if the United States' assertion that their practice represented a consistent series of acts that had been acquiesced to in the region, this practice was not accompanied by any uniform belief that the custom was created. States such as Mexico asserted the doctrine was not legal, even when the attempt was made to include it in treaties such as the Covenant of the League of Nations and other states in the region were reluctant to tie their assent to the Covenant (which occurred for a variety of reasons), to their support for the legal force of the Monroe Doctrine.

Over the period in question there was a legalization of the meaning of the Monroe Doctrine, and unilateral acts more generally, from political statements of policy to precise and binding obligations when state consent could be found. However, it was not clear how a "truly unilateral" statement (to use Fitzmaurice's term) was binding on states unless it was tied to a treaty (as in the *Eastern Greenland Case*) or could be constructed as custom. Further, as the Monroe Doctrine illustrated, there were no formal requirements for how a states' will was to be expressed. In the case of the doctrine, the attempt to find evidence of a custom through regional assent to treaties like the Covenant of the League of Nations was an attempt to construct positive consent to a regional custom.

4 For a basic summary of these two elements of custom, see for example, Thirlway (2010, 101–108).

The history of the Monroe Doctrine has been illustrative of the process of legalization of unilateral acts. Legalization, as I use it, is the process of converting politics to law. Importantly, up to the mid-twentieth century this process of legalization was only conceptualized through the requirement of positive legal assent—the act required consent, it was not simply unilateral.

The tensions the Monroe Doctrine raised, particularly for other states in the region, showed the shortcomings of this consent-based approach. Other states in the Americas clearly contested their consent and the attempt to legalize this obligation beyond its policy origins. The construction of these obligations as an expression of consent (whether to treaty or custom) was a problem when it was understood by non-European (or non-North American) states as an attempt to enforce an obligation in a way that denied their sovereign right to participate in the process of law making.

So, by the middle of the twentieth century unilateral acts had moved from being purely political to potentially legalized obligations through some fancy manoeuvring. However, as the discussion of the Monroe Doctrine indicated, this shift was tenuous at best. It was hard for the United States to demonstrate that they had the required voluntary indications of the will to be bound in the region, and states within the region clearly contested this construction of the doctrine as regional custom. As a result, it was not surprising that by the time of the Cuban Missile Crisis, President Kennedy was given the legal advice that the Monroe Doctrine was a special law, custom, of the region. But it was even less surprising that given the tenuous nature of this construction, he rejected this advice.

As this chapter set out to demonstrate, requiring formal expressions of a will to be bound through tacit consent was the first attempt to legalize unilateral acts. As the Monroe Doctrine illustrated, this approach to unilateral acts was not accepted by all affected states. Moreover, the Monroe Doctrine highlighted a fundamental difficulty with treating unilateral acts as consent-based acts—how could one establish consent in the case of a non-reciprocal act? The only possibility was to interpret consent through other acts (i.e. looking to multilateral treaties) for interpretation. This problem, the need to provide a foundation for unilateral acts within the established sources of law, has been a continual challenge for the legalization of the doctrine. The Monroe Doctrine illustrated that the elasticity provided by implied consent, the lack of precise articulation of what consent might mean, limited the doctrine's application in practice. In other words, legalization at this point was partial because it was imprecise. Chapter 3 picks up on these issues by examining the next attempt to understand the legal nature of unilateral acts.

3 Unilateral Acts as Obligations *Erga Omnes*

The Monroe Doctrine illustrated how the interpretation of unilateral acts changed in between the early nineteenth century and the middle of the twentieth century. When the doctrine was announced it was widely understood that unilateral acts had no legal effect—they were political or diplomatic acts. However, over the course of this time period the understanding of these acts began to shift towards institutionalization within the doctrine.

While the last chapter specifically situated the history of the Monroe Doctrine within the development of international law in the United States, as is fitting for a doctrine that emerged out of American foreign policy, it is worth noting that these developments had parallels within European international law. As Koskenniemi notes in his history of European international law from 1870–1960, there was a specific type of twentieth-century pragmatism that emerged among European international lawyers, such as Lauterpacht, Rolin, or Scelle that included a "commitment to international law as part of the cosmopolitan reason, and projected it as always *already* containing the project of their ideal society" leading them put their faith in a future defined by law (Koskenniemi 2002, 516). As Becker Lorca notes, this pragmatism coincided with a post-war attempt to universalize international law and its history. While this trend had started earlier in the century as non-European states began to be admitted to the community of states, until World War II it also served as a response to what Becker Lorca calls "a new generation of internationalists" who were non-European and who argued for stronger regional international law over a Western-imposed universalism. (See, for example, Alvarez, as discussed in Becker Lorca 2012, 1038–1039.) As a result, through the 1950s, European scholars continued to suggest that any changes to international law were in the quantity of states, not in any essential part of the nature of international law, that and in any case this (pragmatically) reflected universal values and a complete system of law (Koskenniemi, *The Gentle Civilizer of Nations: The Rise and Fall of International Law 1870–1960* 2002, 425; Becker Lorca 2012, 1040–1041).

This trend towards legalized universalism was countered by another post-war trend towards a different pragmatism that was unbounded by either the cosmopolitanism of European international lawyers such as Lauterpacht, or classical American utopianism. This is exemplified by Hans Morgenthau, the German international lawyer who, because of his Jewish heritage, escaped Nazism to settle and teach in the United States, where he would become known as a founder of modern international relations (Koskenniemi, *The Gentle Civilizer of Nations: The Rise and Fall of International Law 1870–1960* 2002, 436–437).

Ironically, Morgenthau, in a full embrace of his new country, adopted the approach of the utopians of the last chapter in tracing his new "realism" to the US "founding fathers" (Koskenniemi, *The Gentle Civilizer of Nations: The Rise and Fall of International Law 1870–1960* 2002, 439–440). Morgenthau's influence, and that of other wartime escapees, on international law (and the new discipline of International Relations) in the United States in the mid-twentieth century was expansive. As Koskenniemi notes, "Political science departments at US Universities received from the German refugees an image of international law as Weimar law writ large, formalistic, moralistic" and ultimately "unable to influence the realities of international life" (Koskenniemi, *The Gentle Civilizer of Nations: The Rise and Fall of International Law 1870–1960* 2002, 471). In international law this led to several responses in the period up to the 1960s. Koskenniemi identifies a specific strain of "rule-scepticism" which led lawyers away from a formalistic study of the classic sources of international law, such as the treaties that were the focus of the last chapter, to the broader "policy choices" of prominent scholars such as McDougal and Lasswell at Yale. This also led to the introduction of an interdisciplinary bent to what had before been the purely doctrinal study of international law (Koskenniemi, *The Gentle Civilizer of Nations: The Rise and Fall of International Law 1870–1960* 2002, 475–476). Even more conservative scholarship began to focus on the causes of conflict or cooperation and non-positivistic approaches to international law (Koskenniemi, *The Gentle Civilizer of Nations: The Rise and Fall of International Law 1870–1960* 2002, 475–479).

The intellectual legacies of World War II were not only felt in international law, but, it has been argued, in diplomacy as well. As the Cold War progressed, American politicians such as President Johnson likened Soviet expansion to pre-World War II German aggression (Roskin 1974, 570). In this, Johnson was continuing President Kennedy's commitment to avoid the mistakes of the Allies in the face of Hitler's provocations through bigger defence budgets, both civilly and internationally, stronger prevention through counterinsurgency and if needed, use of force (Roskin 1974, 573).

So, by the 1970s there was a strange combination of scepticism, pragmatic utopianism, and interdisciplinarity that was shaping international law. As Kennedy has put it,

> Public International Law was to be viewed alternatively as an infant industry [utopianism] and a frail dowager [scepticism], too weak to withstand sustained criticism . . . if it seemed unenforceable, it was a simply a different sort of law ('horizontal' perhaps, like some eccentric cousin who still belonged at family celebrations.
>
> (D. Kennedy 1988–1989, 6)

The effort to legalize unilateral acts was swept up in these trends. As was seen in the previous chapter, the work of scholars such as Schwartzenberger and Fitzmaurice clearly opened the door for international law to regulate unilateral acts. However, the new twentieth-century pragmatism indicated that positivist consent would not be sufficient to regulate this area of law. Consent, the positivists' key concept, could be replaced by a universal conception of unilateral acts as part of the regulation of the conduct of states to prevent future conflicts. As a result, scholars began to think about unilateral acts differently, more universally, as an obligation *erga omnes*, an obligation made by one state to the world at large. This new trend culminated in the 1970s with the *Nuclear Tests Cases* decision.

This decision was called "revolutionary" for its clear determination that "oral statements by government officials—until then unperfected legal acts—could henceforth be deemed binding" (Reisman 2002, 737). Unperfected legal acts were acts in which the legal requirements had not been completed (Black's Law Dictionary 2004). In this way, the *Nuclear Tests Cases* was heralded as establishing the criteria for perfecting unilateral acts, for setting out when unilateral acts could be binding even when it did not indicate consent. This was the next attempt to actualize the notion that unilateral acts were legal obligations; this time in a universal, yet pragmatic, context as obligations *erga omnes* is the subject of the rest of this chapter.

The *Nuclear Tests Cases* and Acts *Erga Omnes*

The *Nuclear Tests Cases* were two separate actions brought before the International Court of Justice (ICJ), the judicial arm of the United Nations, by Australia and New Zealand. The judgments in these actions were so similar that they have generally been discussed together. In these cases, Australia and New Zealand each sued France for testing nuclear weapons above the ground on the Muraroa Atoll in the South Pacific between 1966 and 1972. Australia and New Zealand challenged the legality of these tests on the basis that fallout from the nuclear testing was deposited on their territory and that these tests gave rise to environmental and health concerns. In June 1973, the Court issued an order for interim measures, which enjoined France from further nuclear testing. The French government chose to ignore the interim order and conducted above-ground tests on the atoll in the summer of 1973 and the fall of 1974. Also, France decided not to participate in the proceedings, withdrawing at the preliminary stages on the grounds that the Court had no power to hear the matter (Nuclear Tests Case (Australia v. France) (Judgment) 1974, par 4 ff, paras 17–19).[1]

In absence of French participation the ICJ held that France had made its intentions clear through "a number of authoritative statements" (Nuclear Tests

1 (Nuclear Tests Case (New Zealand v. France) (Judgment), 1974);(Nuclear Tests Case (Australia v. France) (Judgment), 1974). Following convention, these decisions are collectively referred to as the *Nuclear Tests Cases*; all references are to the Australia v. France decision unless otherwise noted.

Case (Australia v. France) (Judgment) 1974, par 20).[2] These statements led the Court to determine that a dispute was present and based on previous diplomatic correspondence to hold that Australia and New Zealand's "object" in the dispute was to have France end its above-ground nuclear testing (Nuclear Tests Case (Australia v. France) (Judgment) 1974, par 24). Constructing the "object" of the dispute in this way allowed the Court to conclude Australia could have understood that the French statements were a "binding" commitment to discontinue nuclear testing. If understood in this way, Australia (and New Zealand) would have felt its "objectives" had been achieved, so that there was no need to proceed any further with the case (Nuclear Tests Case (Australia v. France) (Judgment) 1974, par 27).

If French statements were binding, then France was legally obligated to stop above-ground nuclear testing regardless of the lawsuit against them and Australia and New Zealand's case had no purpose. Consequently, the Court analyzed public statements by French officials closely in order to determine whether these declarations were legally binding. As indicated by the trend towards legalization outlined in the previous chapter, the Court was concerned with whether the statements by French officials indicated any basis for a legal obligation. The Court ultimately concluded, "France made public its intention to cease the conduct of atmospheric nuclear tests following the conclusion of the 1974 series of tests" (Nuclear Tests Case (Australia v. France) (Judgment) 1974, par 41; Nuclear Tests Case (Australia v. France) (Judgment) 1974, paras 34–41).

As a result, the ICJ then considered the legality of these statements, beginning its analysis with a general statement of the law in this area

> It is well recognised that declarations made by way of unilateral acts, concerning legal or factual situations, may have the effect of creating legal obligations. Declarations of this kind may be, and often are, very specific. When it is the intention of the State making the declaration that it should become bound according to its terms, that *intention confers on the declaration the character of a legal undertaking, the State being thenceforth legally required to follow a course of conduct consistent with the declaration.* An undertaking of this kind, if given publicly and with the intent to be bound, even though not made within the context of international negotiations is binding. In these circumstances, *nothing in the nature of a quid pro quo nor any subsequent acceptance of the declaration, nor even any reply*

2 These statements included: a communiqué by the Office of the President of the French Republic, 8 June 1974; a note from the French Embassy in Wellington, New Zealand to the New Zealand Ministry of Foreign Affairs, 10 June 1974; a statement by the President of the French Republic, 25 July 1974; a statement by the Minister of Defence, 16 August 1974; a statement by the Minister of Foreign Affairs in the United Nations General Assembly, 25 September 1974 and a statement by the Minister of Defence, 11 October 1974; (Nuclear Tests Case (Australia v. France) (Judgment), 1974, pp. paras 34–41).

> *or reaction from other states is required* for the declaration to take effect, since such a requirement would be inconsistent with the strictly unilateral nature of the juridical act by which the pronouncement by the state was made.[3]

According to the Court, unilateral acts created a legal obligation when a state expressed its intention that the act was binding. Also, the act had to be autonomous from other acts. No *quid pro quo* or exchange with another state had to take place. These were the core criteria of a "legal" unilateral act: any act of state undertaken with intention to create a legal obligation that was not undertaken for an exchange or a *quid pro quo, but expressed intention*, was legally binding on that state. When these requirements were met, the act could no longer be revoked and the state was legally obligated by its act.

To ascertain when these criteria were met, the Court stated, "intention is to be ascertained by interpretation of the act. When states make statements by which their freedom of action to be limited, a restrictive interpretation is called for" (Nuclear Tests Case (Australia v. France) (Judgment) 1974, par 44). And on this basis the Court concluded that the statements by French officials demonstrated the intention to stop nuclear testing. The ICJ decided, by 9 votes to 6, that the object of the dispute was met. There was no longer a purpose to Australia and New Zealand's claim and so there was no reason to proceed to a decision on the merits of this case (Nuclear Tests Case (Australia v. France) (Judgment) 1974, par 51, 61).

In the *Nuclear Tests Cases* the Court reasoned its way out of ruling on the contentious issue of nuclear testing. This was a pragmatic approach for the Court since it was not likely that France would have recognized the decision and so deciding on this issue would have placed the Court in the awkward position of having produced an unenforceable decision on a contentious issue. This would have damaged the stature of the Court.[4] Instead the ICJ clarified the criteria for unilateral declarations to take legal effect. Any public statement made with the intent to be bound could potentially have legal effect. In stating this conclusion, the Court likely had in mind Schwarzenberger and Fitzmaurice's theories, discussed previously, or at least their spirits, as the Court effectively adopted Schwarzenberger's and Fitzmaurice's two core requirements for a unilateral act to have legal effect. The act had to be autonomous and the state had to intend to be legally bound by their act (Schwarzenberger 1955, 312; Fitzmaurice 1958, 230).

Importantly, these criteria were contested at the time. For example, Australia and New Zealand did not interpret French diplomatic statements as a

3 (Nuclear Tests Case (Australia v. France) (Judgment), 1974, p. par 43) [italics added for emphasis].

4 See, for example, Franck (1975, 612); this also led Franck to highlight the strength and value of the dissenting opinions in this case; (Franck 1975, 613).

substitute for the decision of the Court as, in spite of some earlier statements to the contrary, both countries wanted the ICJ to provide a judgment on the issues (Nuclear Tests (Australia v. France) Memorial on Jurisdiction and Admissibility Submitted by the Government of Australia n.d., Nuclear Tests (Australia v. France) Oral Arguments on Jurisdication and Admissibility: Minutes of Public Sittings n.d., Nuclear Tests (New Zealand v France) Memorial on Jurisdiction and Admissiblity Submitted by the Government of New Zeland n.d., Nuclear Tests (New Zealand v. France) Oral Arguments on Jursidction and Admissibility: Public Sittings n.d.).[5]

As well, some judges were concerned that the Court had radically reinterpreted the submissions of the parties in its decision. The Joint Dissenting Opinion of Judges Onyeama, Dillard, Jiminez de Arechaga, and Waldock noted, "[w]hile the Court is entitled to interpret the submissions of the parties, it is not authorized to introduce into them radical alterations" (Nuclear Tests (New Zealand v. France) Joint Dissenting Opinion (Judgment) 1974, par 10)[6] and, in contrast to the Majority decision, New Zealand was seeking a declaration of illegality and was claiming compensation for past tests. In fact, New Zealand did not just want to stop tests going forward (Nuclear Tests (New Zealand v. France) Joint Dissenting Opinion (Judgment) 1974, paras 13–15), but it also wanted to receive damages for past harms. Limiting New Zealand's right to sue on the basis of French statements made outside the Court changed New Zealand's claim. Arguably, the object of New Zealand's claim was not entirely met.

Additionally, some members of the ICJ felt that French officials had not intended their statements to be binding. In a dissenting opinion Judge (Ad Hoc) Garfield Barwick argued that the Court's interpretation of French statements was "indicative of a failure on the part of the Court to perform" its judicial function. He accepted that France's promises were valid and he acknowledged that New Zealand could always accept a promise by France. New Zealand could also then choose to discontinue the litigation, but they did not. Consequently, Judge Barwick felt that it was not up to the Court to enforce a compromise on the litigant's behalf (Nuclear Tests (New Zealand v. France) Dissenting Opinion, Judge Sir Garfield Barwick (Judgment) 1974, 526–527).

In a similar dissent to the Australian decision Judge Barwick asserted that French statements should have been recognized as findings of fact, not of law. There was "judicial impropriety of deciding the matter without

5 These pleadings contradict the earlier diplomatic negotiations cited by the Court.

6 A similar dissent was appended to the Australian decision with only slight variations to address the differences in the pleadings; a similar argument was advanced in the Separate Opinion of Judge Gros, (Nuclear Tests (Australia v. France) Separate Opinion of Judge Gros (Judgment), 1974, p. par 2). Judge Gros felt Australia had disqualified itself by its conduct (Nuclear Tests (Australia v. France) Separate Opinion of Judge Gros (Judgment), 1974, pp. paras 6, 13).

notice to the Parties of the questions to be considered" (Nuclear Tests (Australia v. France), Dissenting Opinion, Judge Sir Garfield Barwick (Judgment) 1974, 448 ff). This was particularly unfair to France, now legally bound to all nations for all time. Moreover, Judge Barwick was sceptical whether the statements led to the conclusion that France had intended to be bound to such a wide promise (Nuclear Tests (Australia v. France), Dissenting Opinion, Judge Sir Garfield Barwick (Judgment) 1974, 448 ff).

Similarly, Judge de Castro felt it was right to take account of the statements. However, he believed these statements had little "legal worth." He stated, "the fact remains that not every statement of intent is a promise. There is a difference between a promise which gives rise to a moral obligation and a promise which legally binds the promisor" (Nuclear Tests (Australia v. France), Dissenting Opinion, Judge De Castro (Judgment) 1974, par 3), but identifying French intention required evidence. France had to intend to renounce above-ground nuclear testing indefinitely and this standard was not met by the French statements. Consequently, Judge de Castro said, "I see no indication warranting a presumption that France wished to bring into being an international obligation, possessing the same binding force as a treaty—and vis-à-vis whom the whole world?" (Nuclear Tests (Australia v. France), Dissenting Opinion, Judge De Castro (Judgment) 1974, par 4). French statements were primarily evidentiary and were not an indication of a unilateral declaration. Judge de Castro's opinion supported the argument that prior to the *Nuclear Tests Cases* unilateral declarations had been considered similar to treaties, as consent-based obligations. In his opinion, unilateral acts were an obligation to a specific party, not to the world at large. Consequently, Judge de Castro's dissent supported the view that *Nuclear Tests Cases* fundamentally reshaped the law as the decision created new criteria for legalization of unilateral acts. The criteria of intention and autonomy were novel.

The *Nuclear Tests Cases* also established a new doctrinal basis for unilateral acts. The Court now tied the legal effect of unilateral acts to the principle of good faith, moving away from consent. The decision stated:

> One of the basic principles governing the creation and performance of legal obligations, whatever their source, is the principle of good faith. Trust and confidence are inherent in international co-operation, in particular in an age when this co-operation in many fields is becoming increasingly essential. Just as the very rule of *pacta sunt servanda* in the law of treaties is based on good faith, so also is the binding character of an international obligation assumed by unilateral declaration. Thus interested states may take cognizance of unilateral declarations and place confidence in them, and are entitled to require that the obligation thus created be respected.
>
> (Nuclear Tests Case (Australia v. France) (Judgment) 1974, par 46)

Here, the ICJ echoed Schwarzenberger's assertion of *contra factum*, the principle that one cannot make a contrary assertion, which resulted in the Court's determination that a unilateral act was binding in good faith. Consequently, states could now rely on unilateral acts made in good faith.

However, the requirement of good faith was problematic because, as will be discussed in later chapters, it tried to separate formal unilateral acts from any type of reliance on that act. Unilateral acts were all autonomous acts, as Fitzmaurice had required. But autonomy was going to be difficult to prove in practice. It also led to other questions that were considered by the Court: When was a state entitled to change their intention? Was a unilateral act revocable? In the *Nuclear Tests Cases* the ICJ held that the "unilateral undertaking resulting from these statements cannot be interpreted as having been made in implicit reliance on arbitrary power of reconsideration" (Nuclear Tests Case (Australia v. France) (Judgment) 1974, par 51). In this way the decision limited a state's ability to change a unilateral act and so this case has stood for the proposition that unilateral acts could not be revoked arbitrarily.

In sum, this case formalized three things. First, it institutionalized unilateral acts as a formal category in the doctrine. Second, it delimited the criteria for unilateral acts; it clarified that a unilateral act required intention, autonomy, and revocation. Of these three criteria, intention was the primary requirement for a unilateral act to become formally binding, although the Court did not establish how to determine intention except in the most general terms (Nuclear Tests Case (Australia v. France) (Judgment) 1974, par 43). Third, it held that once the state unilaterally accepted an obligation it was universally binding—*erga omnes*. This final requirement made the other two elements of the decision more precise, making it necessary to divert attention for a bit to explain obligations *erga omnes*.

Obligations *Erga Omnes*

The concept of obligations *erga omnes* has been problematic for the doctrine of international law. The notion of obligation *erga omnes* was of twentieth-century origin, gaining formal recognition at the ICJ as an aside in a judgment of the International Court of Justice, the *Barcelona Traction Case*, in 1970. In this case the Court introduced the idea of an obligation *erga omnes* as a legal obligation "towards the international community as a whole" which were the "concern of all states" and of such importance that the rights inherent in them must be protected by all states. These obligations, the decision clarified, arose from both the "outlawing" of aggression and genocide and other peremptory norms such as the prohibition on slavery and the introduction of universal or nearly universal treaties (Case Concerning the Barcelona Traction, Light and Power Company (Belgium v. Spain, Second Phase) Judgment [1970] ICJ Rep 3 n.d., par 33). This sounds straightforward but as Tams has noted, "there is no agreement about the scope of the *erga omnes* concept and the legal consequences flowing from that status remain unclear" (Tams, Enforcing Obligations Erga Omnes in International Law 2005, 4).

Additionally, this decision was controversial. The argument was made that the statements in *Barcelona Traction* were *dicta*, statements that were not directed to the main substance of a decision. There has been debate about the binding weight of *dicta* in international law, as it is not settled whether international law distinguishes between parts of a decision in the way that common law does, but there has been some support for the proposition that not all parts of a decision have to be given equal legal weight (Ragazzi 2000, 6–7, Tams, Enforcing Obligations Erga Omnes in International Law 2005, 168–171). A second objection, similar to this first one, was that the Court in *Barcelona Traction* was not clear in its elucidation of the concept of obligations *erga omnes* and so it was not of much precedential value. However, the subsequent development of this concept has made this objection increasingly less relevant (Ragazzi 2000, 17; Tams, Enforcing Obligations Erga Omnes in International Law 2005, 165–168).[7]

Importantly, as Ragazzi has noted, the *Barcelona Traction Case* identified two core requirements of an obligation *erga omnes*; they had to be universal since they were "binding on all states without exception" and they had to express international "solidarity" since they assumed that all states would have an interest in the protection of these principles (Ragazzi 2000, 17).

The concept of obligations *erga omnes* was first applied to unilateral acts in the *Nuclear Tests Cases* when the parties pled that a prohibition on atmospheric nuclear testing did not require proof of actual damages from the testing. Australia and New Zealand both set out to prove that there was a rule of customary international law forbidding atmospheric nuclear testing and that this rule was a result of an obligation *erga omnes*. They then argued that this obligation was opposable against France. Although this was not actually addressed in the decision, four of the dissenting opinions did try to establish a general right to bring a claim on the basis of an obligation *erga omnes* (Tams, Enforcing Obligations Erga Omnes in International Law 2005, 180–182).[8]

However, in the *Nuclear Tests Cases* the majority did not directly address the issue of a right to bring a claim under obligations *erga omnes* and the Court was ambiguous about whether all states could hold France to their obligation going forward. This was because, in contrast to the intent in the *Barcelona Traction* decision, the majority in the *Nuclear Tests Cases* used the concept of obligations *erga omnes* to establish why French statements made "to the world at large" were binding when Australia and New Zealand, the parties to the case, already had the right to bring a claim. This reversal of the scenario in the *Barcelona Traction Case* led Tams to conclude that the Court used the term *erga omnes* descriptively and it did not have legal consequences. In this sense,

7 Tams raises four other objections, but these seem to be the two main ones for purposes of this work.

8 As Tams noted correctly these discussions appear in the Dissents of Judges De Castro, Barwick, and Joint Dissenting Opinions of Onyema, Dillard, Jiminez de Arechaga and Waldock.

the Court used the phrase in a general sense to refer "to all states" (Tams, Enforcing Obligations Erga Omnes in International Law 2005, 114–115; Nuclear Tests Case (Australia v. France) (Judgment) 1974, paras 49–52).

As a result of the vagueness of the concept of obligations *erga omnes*, authors have tried to parse the relationship between these obligations and *jus cogens*, fundamental norms of international law from which states could not depart. What has been debated is whether obligations *erga omnes* were a form of *jus cogens* or a procedure that gave rise to a claim before a court as a form of state responsibility (Bassiouni 1996; Byers 1997; Rubin 2001; Vermeer-Kunzli 2007; Tams and Asteriti, Erga Omnes, Jus Cogens, and their Impact on the Law of Responsibility 2013). Theoretically, if obligations *erga omnes* were fundamental norms, then states could invoke these acts because no state could depart from them and they were enforceable by any state. On the other hand, if obligations *erga omnes* are a form of state responsibility, then obligations *erga omnes* could create a right to bring a claim, called standing, before the ICJ (as well as other possible remedial measures) (Tams and Asteriti, Erga Omnes, Jus Cogens, and their Impact on the Law of Responsibility 2013) in order to enforce the state's responsibility.

What is the difference between a *jus cogens* and *erga omnes*? The answer lies in the idea of "derogability," the ability of states to dissent from these rules. As Byers has argued, *jus cogens* nullify any rules that contradict them, so there can be no dissenting from these rules. In contrast, if *erga omnes* rules are rules of standing, they are only procedural rules that establish a right to bring a claim. As a result, some scholars have suggested that *erga omnes* and *jus cogens* are two sides of the same concept, while others have said that *erga omnes* have a wider scope than *jus cogens* (Byers 1997, 211, 230–231; Bassiouni 1996, 63).

However, this debate has been purely theoretical. Since the *Barcelona Traction* decision, it has been an open question whether or not the obligations *erga omnes* gave rise to a right to bring a claim before the ICJ. In fact, Tams has observed that the Court has never permitted a claim based on *erga omnes* standing. This may result from the fact that the Court's jurisdiction can arise out of consent by a state. The various dissenting decisions to the *Nuclear Tests Cases* seem to take for granted that consent exists (Tams, Enforcing Obligations Erga Omnes in International Law 2005, 158–160, 180–181; Nuclear Tests Case (Australia v. France) (Judgment) 1974).

In sum: obligations *erga omnes*, obligations to the world at large, have been related to universal obligations such as *jus cogens*. But this is not the only meaning since the obligations created in the *Nuclear Tests Cases*, were clearly not *jus cogens* norms. From this it can be concluded, as Tams did above, that France's promise was not to the world at large; the use of the term *erga omnes* was descriptive and without legal consequences. So, while obligation *erga omnes* could, theoretically, create a legalized obligation, this has not been applied in practice.

The *Nuclear Tests Cases* defined unilateral acts as obligations *erga omnes*, but this is not a well-defined concept. Obligations *erga omnes* have been defined as consent-based obligations, creating standing, or as universal obligations, *jus cogens*. This core definitional problem, as we shall see, has impacted greatly on the potential for legalization of unilateral acts.

The Problem with Identifying Unilateral Acts That Were Obligations *Erga Omnes*

According to the criteria from the *Nuclear Tests Cases*, a unilateral act becomes legalized when a state expresses an intention to create an obligation. Once intention is present, the act becomes binding on that state in good faith. Formally, the act does not have to be addressed to a specific state in order to create an obligation, as it is the acting state's intention that defines the obligation. And, because they do not need to be addressed to any other state in particular, these acts have been classified as an obligation *erga omnes*. But, explaining unilateral acts through the imprecise category of obligations *erga omnes* made it difficult to identify when a unilateral act existed.

In fact, there were three specific problems with the criteria the *Nuclear Tests Cases* established. First, there were difficulties in identifying a state's intention, second, there were problems with determining when the act is autonomous, and third, there were issues surrounding when these acts could be revoked.

Intention

Intention was necessary for a unilateral act to create a legal obligation. However, intention is a state of mind, which means that it is difficult to observe, as there is no outward evidence of a legal obligation. Consequently, in order for the Court to reach the conclusion it reached in the *Nuclear Tests Cases*, it had to make intention capable of observation.

Kennedy has noted that in the *Nuclear Tests Cases* the Court had to determine "the way in which another state could be expected to view French statements" (D. Kennedy 1987, 53). This was particularly important given the formulation of these acts as obligations to the world at large, while at the same time it was the subject of a lawsuit between specific parties. Koskenniemi reiterated this point when he analyzed the decision and observed that:

> [t]he strategy in the *Nuclear Tests Case* is to give effect to all three considerations: Subjective French intent, subjective reliance by Australia and objective justice. Each renders the same solution: France is bound. No preference is made. But the argument leaves unexplained how the court can maintain that it gives effect to French intent in face of the fact that France denied it. It leaves unexplained how it can protect the Applicant's reliance as they deny having relied. And it leaves unexplained its theory of justice, which says that certain statements bind by virtue of good faith. Moreover, having recourse to the three arguments is contradictory. Each of them makes the other two superfluous. If giving effect to French intent is what counts, then it must suffice as the sole criterion: its point is to override

> other State's intent or objective justice. And if justice is effectual it must override any subjective intent or reliance.
>
> (Koskenniemi, From Apology to Utopia: The Structure of International Legal Argument n.d., 354)

Koskenniemi suggested that in the *Nuclear Tests Cases* the Court paid lip service to intention as the key requirement of a unilateral act while at the same time using language that allowed them to ignore the actual intention of the acting state. This was possible because intention was a subjective concept, which was internal to the acting state so that it could not be determined without interpretation. The act created a legal obligation when an opposed party could identify the acting state's intention objectively, that is through an external expression of their intentions. Further, the act had to be formulated in such a way that anyone looking at the act could reasonably believe the state was now obligated by its intention in good faith. To rephrase, a unilateral act gained legal authority when there was evidence to indicate that the state had consented to give the act legal authority. There was no practical way to identify a state's intention other than through the objective analysis of the act itself. But, this brought out the same problems with using consent as the basis for legalizing unilateral act that were explored in Chapter 2.

Intention also created another problem, which can be exemplified by the concrete example of the *Nuclear Tests Cases*: If French statements manifested France's intention, why did Australia and New Zealand institute their claim? To Australia and New Zealand, French actions did not confirm French intentions. So, according to the decision, a restrictive interpretation of the act was called for, and on this approach, there was no obligation present. This suggests a second difficulty with applying intention in this context—that in order for an individual act to display objective indications of intention, other states had to see evidence that the intention to create an obligation was obvious from the act. And this was not the case for Australia and New Zealand or they would not have sued France.

Autonomy

Autonomy, the idea that an obligation was not premised on reciprocal obligations (as in a tacit treaty), was a necessary step towards defining a unilateral act as an obligation *erga omnes*. If an act did not need to have an addressee, then it was not necessarily a result of reciprocal legal obligations.

The *Nuclear Tests Cases* made autonomy a requirement of unilateral acts (Nuclear Tests Case (Australia v. France) (Judgment) 1974, par 43). Before this decision, there was no consensus that a unilateral act created an autonomous legal obligation as earlier case law did not consider this issue directly (A. Rubin 1977, 3–7).[9] For example, in the *Eastern Greenland Case*, which

9 Further, Garner, in his 1933 article on the unilateral declarations, discussed the leading precursor to the *Nuclear Tests cases*, the *Eastern Greenland case*. In his analysis he appeared to treat unilateral declarations as a form of oral agreement; see generally, (Garner, The

was discussed briefly in the previous chapter, the Court considered the Danish response to the statement of the Norwegian Foreign Minister. This response took place in the context of ongoing negotiations (Hudson n.d., 151ff; Franck 1975) and as a result the PCIJ considered the act reciprocal in nature. So, it was a doctrinal shift when, in the *Nuclear Tests Cases*, the ICJ stated that,

> An undertaking of this kind, if given public, and with an intent to be bound, even though not made within the context of international negotiations is binding. In these circumstances nothing in the nature of a *quid pro quo* nor any subsequent acceptance of the declaration, nor even any reply or reaction from other states, is required for the declaration to take effect, since a requirement would be inconsistent with the strictly unilateral nature of the juridical act by which the pronouncement by the state was made.
> (Nuclear Tests Case (Australia v. France) (Judgment) 1974, par 43)

In this paragraph, the Court set out the way in which unilateral acts could create legal obligation, by excluding any formalities or response by other states. The lack of response by other states made unilateral acts different from contracts, since there was no requirement of consideration, as in common law obligations, or a requirement of cause, as in civil law obligations. The only requirement was intention to be bound by the act, whether or not that act was "synallagmatic," reciprocal (Thirlway 1990, 12–13). In brief: The requirement of autonomy formally separated unilateral acts from other consent-based obligations

So, theoretically, states undertaking unilateral acts were not concerned with the reaction of other states to their act and so there was no need for any sort of interaction with other states in order for a unilateral act to be considered binding (Nuclear Tests Case (Australia v. France) (Judgment) 1974, par 43). However, in the *Nuclear Tests Cases* decision the Court also stated that:

> [t]rust and confidence are inherent in international co-operation, in particular in an age when this co-operation in many fields is becoming increasingly essential. Just as the very rule of *pacta sunt servanda* in the law of treaties is based on good faith, so also is the binding character of an international obligation assumed by unilateral declaration. Thus interested states may take cognizance of unilateral declarations and place confidence in them, and are entitled to require that the obligation thus created be respected.
> (Nuclear Tests Case (Australia v. France) (Judgment) 1974, par 46)

This was contradictory. On the one hand, the Court required that the unilateral declaration was autonomous. An obligation could be created without any response, recognition, or even acknowledgement of the act by other states.

International Binding Force of Unilateral Oral Declarations, 1933). Verzijil offers case law examples of unilateral declarations held to binding, however in his analysis these acts are all contextualized, and are not autonomous acts (Verzijil 1973, 107–109).

On the other hand, the Court explained the need for autonomy by raising the requirement of good faith in the international arena. Good faith, in theory, promoted cooperation between states by ensuring that a state's word will be kept.

The requirement of autonomy created a paradox. Unilateral acts were autonomous in order to ensure that states placed their faith in the obligation the act created. However, the fact that good faith was introduced to encourage trust implied that some response on the part of other states was needed to identify a unilateral act. Intention was not enough to guarantee that a unilateral act would be kept. This paradox, that the autonomous act required a response, raised several further questions: Could an autonomous act ever be undertaken in concert with other states? If a state acted unilaterally, how could that act ever require a response on the part of other states?

In the *Nuclear Tests Cases* the ICJ avoided all these logical conundrums. The Court had before it a concrete case in which Australia and New Zealand were responding to France's actions. The Court was able to construct an obligation from France's statements without having to explicitly consider whether these statements required a response from Australia and New Zealand (Nuclear Tests Case (Australia v. France) (Judgment) 1974, par 46). As a result, the issue of standing *erga omnes* was not effectively resolved. However, if Australia and New Zealand had not noticed France's nuclear tests and had not claimed damages as a result, there would have been no claim for the Court to hear. The consequence of this vagueness was that both reaction and trust effectively became requirements of unilateral acts.

Koskenniemi has raised this point in relation to the *Nuclear Tests Cases.* He asserted that:

> [t]he judgment followed the strategy of tacit consent, French intent was construed on the basis of the status of the authorities involved, the "general nature and characteristic of these statements" and the fact that they were addressed to the public at large. These same facts also made it possible to appeal to the subjective reliance of other States and to non-subjective considerations about good faith, trust and confidence etc.
>
> (Koskenniemi, From Apology to Utopia: The Structure of International Legal Argument n.d., 352)

Therefore, as Kosekenniemi pointed out, the ICJ's decision was not, in actuality, doctrinally different from the older cases that relied on tacit consent, with all the problems this entails. The ICJ implicitly considered Australia and New Zealand's reaction to the French statements. The Court tried to make the unilateral act meet the needs of Australia and New Zealand as well as France. As Franck noted, "[i]ntentionality as the Court said, must be the test. But intention cannot be determined solely by reference to the speaker's state of mind, but must also take into account that of the listeners." (Franck 1975, 616). This observation was borne out by the fact that the Court in effect gave credence to the views of Australia and New Zealand when evaluating French actions. Practically, France's obligations were determined by the good faith placed in the act by Australia and New Zealand. France's own reasons for adhering to the act are never determined (Nuclear Tests Case (Australia v. France) (Judgment) 1974). The Court, in effect, made a reaction a primary consideration in the determination of a unilateral obligation.

This *de facto* requirement of a reaction to the unilateral act resulted from a conundrum the Court faced, which could be termed the "the tree falls in the forest" problem. If a unilateral act was truly autonomous, then no response to the act was required in order for the act to be considered legal. If states did not respond to a unilateral act, the act became similar to a tree that fell in the forest that no one heard. Did the act make a sound? Did it create a legal obligation? As with the proverbial tree, the answer was, theoretically, yes. However, like the fallen tree, the obligatory force of a unilateral act could not be determined without, at a minimum, a reaction to the act by another state. So, without some reaction by another state, it was impossible to know whether a formal unilateral act was created.

This problem is further clarified by the following hypothetical example: suppose Spain made a statement that it was going to allow a referendum on the sovereignty of Catalonia. At this point, this act had no international legal impact since Spain had never recognized Catalan independence. This was an internal act of Spanish law with international implications, but at this point it was not clear if Spain intended to create an obligation under international law or if Spain intended to create a new political policy. In effect, the legality of Spain's statement had not been determined yet. If Spain then held the referendum as it had promised, then the act continued to have this nebulous legal status. If, however, Spain cancelled the referendum, then the legality of this act could be determined because once the referendum was cancelled other states could respond to this broken promise in order to hold Spain to its word. Good faith then became a priority, and states were able to put pressure on Spain to comply with its obligation. For example, states could send a reference question on the issue to the ICJ. It is only at this point that the legality of Spain's statement would be considered. Consequently, it was not until other states "heard" or had some kind of reaction to Spain's act that its legality could be assessed. However, this requirement of a reaction challenged the idea that the act was autonomous since the unilateral act was considered legal only when another state reacted to the act. Conversely, when there was no reaction to the act, it was impossible to determine whether the act created a legal obligation because it is still considered a purely domestic political act. So, like the tree that fell in the forest, a unilateral act may make a sound, but if no one "hears" that sound then the act does not create a legal obligation (Koskenniemi, From Apology to Utopia: The Structure of International Legal Argument n.d.).

This example demonstrates the core contradiction in the requirement of autonomy. And, arguably, it is this contradiction that has forced the court to state that unilateral acts are subject to claims of good faith. Good faith is the "trust" required for international cooperation. However, there can be no "trust" without a reaction to an act because good faith only becomes an issue when another state raises a claim about the legality of the unilateral act. As the previous example demonstrates, a state must be able to show that it has "heard" and placed trust in the act in order to argue that the promise must be upheld. This meant that, in practice, a state has to show, at a minimum, that it has reacted to and placed trust in the act in some way in order for the act to be binding. This requirement made it difficult to find an autonomous act, and it also has made it hard to separate unilateral acts hard from other obligations based on good faith.

Good faith has been considered a general principle of international law, a universal norm necessary to all legal systems and so by introducing this concept, the ICJ was trying to balance the sovereign's ability to bind itself with the need for a reaction by other states in order for the act to have effect outside of the acting state, to make an international and not a domestic act (Nuclear Tests Case 1974).

Franck disagreed. Franck argued that paying attention to the listener's understanding of intention did not translate into a requirement of a quid pro quo, a need for states to respond to the act. He argued that this was so because the Court did not adopt the speaker's, France's, intent. Nor did it adopt the listeners', Australia's and New Zealand's, intention. It constructed its own intention. While this was true and, theoretically, as the Spanish example demonstrated, it was possible to separate the requirement for cooperation from the acting state's intention, practically his argument is weak. Put simply, if Australia and New Zealand hadn't reacted to France's act, there would have been no case for the Court to hear. As a result, Koskenniemi has argued that the construction of intention always begins with a reaction by another state or there is a trial at a Court that is actively constructing this intention (Franck, 1975, and Koskenniemi, nd).

The *Nuclear Tests Cases* illustrated that an obligation was not created without some form of reaction to the act and that that act is trusted by other states. And once a reaction was trusted by other states the act became binding in good faith. This contradiction in the doctrine made it difficult to say that unilateral acts were purely autonomous acts (Koskenniemi, From Apology to Utopia: The Structure of International Legal Argument n.d., 354).[10] This tension in unilateral acts, between autonomy and reaction, between the sovereign right of a state to bind itself through its will and the universal requirement of intent, has also been linked to the final requirement for a unilateral act, revocation.

Revocation

The *Nuclear Tests Cases* established that unilateral acts were not automatically revocable. As the Court stated, the "unilateral undertaking resulting from [the French] statements cannot be interpreted as having been made in an implicit

10 This was premised on Koskenniemi's assertion that unilateral acts will always lack the certainty to be distinguished from political obligations.

reliance on arbitrary power of reconsideration" (Nuclear Tests Case (Australia v. France) (Judgment) 1974, par 51). The principle of revocability was limited further by the requirement that it was not arbitrary, but the ICJ did not explain what would constitute arbitrariness or, alternatively what would constitute legitimate termination.

Importantly, since this decision the ICJ has applied the limit on arbitrary revocation of unilateral acts in other cases. Through these decisions, it has become clearer what this limit meant. For example, revocation was an issue in the *Case Concerning Military and Paramilitary Activities in and Against Nicaragua*. In this case the Court considered whether the United States "modification" of its declaration of acceptance of the jurisdiction of the Court under Article 36(2) of the Statute of ICJ was valid. The Court held that it was not. The Court acknowledged that the United States had the right to modify its obligation and further, the Court asserted that this right was inherent in any unilateral act.[11] However, the ICJ went on to suggest that good faith required the United States to uphold its commitments regarding the jurisdiction of the Court. In this case the Court interpreted arbitrariness to include a general right to revoke a unilateral undertaking but limited this right by stating that revocation could not violate another principle of law such as good faith (Military and Paramilitary Activities in and Against Nicaragua (Nicaragua v. United States of America) (Judgment, Jurisdiction) 1984, par. 62–63).

Revocation was also considered in the *Fisheries Jurisdiction Case*. In this case the Court was asked to interpret Canada's reservation to its declaration accepting the jurisdiction of the ICJ under Article 36(2). In this case the Court confirmed that acceptance of the ICJ's jurisdiction was a unilateral act. However, it also argued that this act was not autonomous, it created a relationship with other depository states, and this could create trust in other states so the act could not be unilaterally revoked or changed (Fisheries Juridiction Case (Spain v. Canada) (Judgment -Jurisdiction) 1998, paras 42, 46).

These two cases at the ICJ indicate that there is a general rule that unilateral acts are revocable unless they are limited by good faith. And good faith has meant that states had a duty to live up to their obligations and they are prevented from arbitrarily revoking their unilateral acts. However, good faith only exists when there is trust placed in the unilateral act. This point was underscored by Major Bulman who wrote that, "[f]irst, and most importantly,

11 As the decision stated:

> Although the United States retained the right to modify the contents of the 1946 Declaration or to terminate it, a power which is inherent in any unilateral act of State, it has, nevertheless assumed an inescapable obligation towards other States accepting the Optional Clause, by stating formally and solemnly that any such change should take effect only six months have elapsed from the date of notice.

(Military and Paramilitary Activities in and Against Nicaragua (Nicaragua v. United States of America) (Judgment, Jurisdiction, 1984, p. par 61).

the court underscored the potential legal dangers for states that issue unilateral declarations and then subsequently repudiate them" (Bulman 1999, 161).

In the *Nuclear Tests Cases* and subsequent decisions, the ICJ has confirmed that states have the right to revoke their unilateral acts. And, in theory, this meant that states could determine that their intention had changed and they could revoke their act. This was necessary to protect the autonomy of the act but, as was demonstrated above, these acts were never really autonomous, and the ICJ has not protected them as if they are. The ICJ limited the acting state's right to revoke their unilateral act based on the reaction other states had to the act and the trust these reacting states placed in the act. Put another way, the right of sovereign states to revoke their unilateral acts was limited in order ensure that these acts had the trust necessary to give them legal authority.

Unilateral Acts as Unilateral Acts *Erga Omnes* Since the *Nuclear Tests Cases*

Since the *Nuclear Tests Cases*, several prominent cases have applied the decision,[12] and all of these cases have demonstrated the difficulties with treating unilateral acts as obligations *erga omnes*. In the intervening years the ICJ has not made sense of the contradictory requirements of intention, autonomy, and revocability.

The first case to apply the *Nuclear Tests Cases* has already been mentioned briefly. The *Military and Paramilitary Activities in and Against Nicaragua Case* arose out of the United States' covert intervention in Nicaragua. In the 1980s the United States began providing "training advice and support" to the Contra guerrilla fighters, fighters who were opposed to the communist-leaning government of Nicaragua. This government had taken power in a revolt by the Sandinista rebels, which in turn lead to the fall of the Somoza dictatorship, in 1979–1980 (Gill 1989, 199ff).

In response to the United States' interference, Nicaragua filed a claim at the ICJ and requested an order to require the United States to stop intervening in Nicaraguan affairs. They also claimed damages. The United States tried to block the litigation by issuing a statement that became known as the "Schultz Declaration." In this declaration the United States retroactively rescinded their consent to the jurisdiction of the Court. On this basis, the United States tried to have Nicaragua's claim removed from the Court's list. They argued that the Court did not have jurisdiction to hear the merits of the case. The Court did not accept these arguments and consequently the United States withdrew from the litigation (Gill 1989, 210, 217–219).

12 Other cases have tangentially dealt with similar issues, such as the (Case Concerning Border and Transborder Armed Actions (Nicaragua v. Honduras) (Judgment), 1988); and; (Aegean Sea Continental Shelf Case (Greece v. Turkey) (Judgment), 1978) These cases do not directly pertain to the present discussion; see, for example, Kwiatkowska (1995).

This decision forced the United States to justify its interference in Nicaragua. The United States argued that they took action because the Nicaraguan Government was ignoring its "'solemn commitments to the Nicaraguan people, the United States and the Organisation of American States'" to institute a democratic government, including elections (Military and Paramilitary Activities in and Against Nicaragua (Nicaragua v. United States of America) (Judgment, Merits) 1986, par 257; Thirlway 1990, 17–18). As a result the ICJ had to determine if Nicaragua had made a unilateral promise to transition to a democratic form of government and hold elections. This argument was not addressed by Nicaragua in its pleadings or oral arguments (Case Concerning Military and Paramilitary Activities in and Against Nicaragua (Nicaragua v. USA) ICJ Oral Pleadings 2007, 18; Case Concerning Military and Paramilitary Activities in and Against Nicaragua (Nicaragua v. Usa) Memorial of Nicaragua (Merits) n.d., Case Concerning Military and Paramilitary Activities in and Against Nicaragua (Nicaragua v. USA) ICJ Oral Pleadings 2007). Instead, the Court held on the evidence that the promise to have elections was a domestic act, not an international act. The Court did not find any evidence of a unilateral act by Nicaragua and the ICJ was not prepared to entertain this promise as an obligation as *erga omnes*. Interestingly, the Court did not refer directly to the *Nuclear Tests Cases* and instead they asserted that even if the Nicaraguan government made this promise, it was to the Organization of American States, not to the United States. Additionally, the Court did not try to assess the intention of a state undertaking an autonomous legal act, instead it examined a unilateral obligation undertaken between specific parties and found that no such obligation existed (Military and Paramilitary Activities in and Against Nicaragua (Nicaragua v. United States of America) (Judgment, Merits) 1986, 27, 31,58, 71, 260–262; Thirlway 1990, 18).

The second case that considered unilateral acts was the *Case Concerning the Frontier Dispute* between Burkina Faso and Mali. This case emerged out of a border dispute between these two countries. To resolve this dispute, a Mediation Commission was set up and in the course of the work of this Commission the Head of State of Mali stated that they would consider the recommendations of the Mediation Commission binding, even though this body had not been given binding powers. As a result, the Court considered whether this Malian statement had legal effect. In fact, Mali denied that they had intended the statements to have legal effect and called them a "witticism" (Case Concerning the Frontier Dispute (Burkina Faso v. Mali) (Judgment) 1986).

In analyzing these arguments the Court determined that Mali's statements were not made in the context of negotiations. As a result, the Court considered the statements similar to French statements in the *Nuclear Tests Cases*. However, again in this decision, the ICJ narrowed the interpretation of intention; they stated that intention was established in the same circumstances as in the *Nicaragua Case*. As a result, The Court took a cautious approach and found that non-directed statements, such as the general statements of Mali's Head of State, were not legally binding. The Court differentiated this case from the *Nuclear Tests Cases* by holding that in that case the broad subject matter and the situation of the parties to the litigation had necessitated an *erga omnes* statement. In this case the Court felt the parties had the option of reaching an agreement. And it was only within this context that Mali intended to be bound by their statements (Case Concerning the Frontier Dispute (Burkina Faso v. Mali) (Judgment) 1986, paras 38–40; Thirlway 1990, 18).[13]

This case demonstrated the difficulty the Court had constructing intention from non-directed statements. In this case the ICJ did not rely on Mali's intent (the "witticism") or Burkina Faso's claim of reliance but constructed intention from the fact that the parties could have reached an agreement. The fact that the Court constructed Mali's intention in this way illustrates how difficult the Court has found it to apply the concept of an obligation *erga omnes* to a unilateral act. The Court chose to avoid these difficulties by ignoring Mali's claim to sovereignty and Burkina Faso's claim to reliance and instead they returned to the older conception of a less than autonomous act, a consent-based obligation found in the *Eastern Greenland Case.*

The third case in which unilateral acts were considered was the *Case Concerning Sovereignty over Pedra Branca/Pulau Batu Puteh, Middle Rocks and South Ledge.* In this case the ICJ considered sovereignty over Pedra Branca/ Pulau Batu Puteh Island, which was a source of friction between Malaysia and Singapore. The Parties agreed that the dispute "crystallized" in 1980 when Singapore protested publication of maps showing Malaysian sovereignty over Pedra Branca/Pulau Batu Puteh Island, although it was less clear when the dispute over the middle rocks and south ledge of the Island began, so the Court settled on 1993 as the date of crystallization of the latter claim (Case Concerning Sovereignty over Pedra Branca/ Pulau Batu Puteh, Middle Rocks and South Ledge (Malaysia v. Singapore) (Judgment) [2008] List No 130 n.d.).

The court was concerned with correspondence from 1953 between Singapore and the British Advisor to the Sultan of Johor (in Malaysia) that asked him to confirm sovereignty over Pedra Branca/Pulau Batu Puteh. The reply that was written by the Acting Secretary of State for Johor disclaimed ownership over the Island. The parties interpreted this letter, known as the Johor reply, in various ways; Malaysia argued the letter disclaimed "ownership," not sovereignty, or alternatively that the latter was written without authority. Singapore claimed that the letter disclaimed title and, as a result, sovereignty over the Island. The ICJ held that the letter was not a disclaimer of title to the Island, and that Singapore could not prove that there had been the detrimental reliance necessary to estop Malaysia in its claim (Case Concerning

13 Thirlway also discussed the *Border and Transborder Armed Action Case* between Nicaragua and Honduras, but this is in the context of his discussion of good faith. The "declaration" discussed in this case was analogous to a treaty obligation (Thirlway H., 1990, 20–21).

Sovereignty over Pedra Branca/ Pulau Batu Puteh, Middle Rocks and South Ledge (Malaysia v. Singapore) (Judgment) [2008] List No 130 n.d.).

Finally, the Court considered the unilateral nature of the "Johor reply." The Court acknowledged that the statement was made without reference to a claim or dispute with Singapore and so, they held, it did not indicate a unilateral obligation. According to the ICJ, the "Johor reply" was just an answer to a question posed by Singapore and was not an indication of a legal obligation that affected sovereignty over Pedra Branca/Pulau Batu Puteh. Therefore, the ICJ decided that there was no unilateral act in this case (Case Concerning Sovereignty over Pedra Branca/ Pulau Batu Puteh, Middle Rocks and South Ledge (Malaysia v. Singapore) (Judgment) [2008] List No 130 n.d., paras 33–36, 192, 193,197–201, 222–226,229–230).

Most recently, the ICJ has considered unilateral action in the case of the *Accordance with International Law of the Unilateral Declaration of Independence by the Provisional Institutions of Self-Government of Kosovo*, in which the UN General Assembly asked for an advisory opinion on the unilateral declaration of independence of Kosovo. This decision will be discussed in more detail later in this book, in Chapter 6. Additionally, the Working Group of the ILC considered the topic of unilateral acts suited for codification because it had been considered in the jurisprudence, particularly in the *Nuclear Tests Cases.* This case was also the source of the criteria used in the typology the ILC proposed for its study of unilateral acts (ILC Yearbook 1996 n.d., addendum 3, paras 3, 8).These criteria and the relationship to the work of the ILC will be discussed in further detail in Chapter 5.[14]

The review of subsequent case law demonstrates the central role of the *Nuclear Tests Cases* in the discourse of unilateral acts. Following the *Nuclear Tests Cases*, unilateral acts were defined as any act that meets the criteria of intention, autonomy, and revocation. Moreover, when an act has been found to be legally binding, it has been binding not to a specific state, but as an obligation to all states, universally, as an obligation *erga omnes.* However, the case law has also demonstrated the difficulties with applying this discourse in practice.

14 This has also been raised in oral arguments before the ICJ. See, for example, Questions Relating to the Obligation to Prosecute or Extradite (Senegal v. Belgium), CR 2012/5 available online at www.icj-cij.org accessed on 11 December 2015; Maritime Dispute (Chile v. Peru), CR 2012/34 available online at www.icj-cij.org, accessed on 11 December 2015. The final decision also raised the topic of unilateral declarations, Also see, Maritime Dispute (Peru v. Chile), Judgment of 24 January 2014, available online at www.icj-cij.org accessed on 22 March 2018. A Guzman Escobar, "Bolivia's Resasonably Strong Case against Chile" *Opinio Juris* (21 March 2014) at http://opiniojuris.org/2014/03/21/bolivias-reasonably-strong-icj-case-chile/ accessed on 22 March 2018.

Unilateral Act as Obligation *Erga Omnes*: The Creation of a Universal Obligation

The *Nuclear Tests Cases* presented a problem for the Court. The ICJ faced a contentious case on a controversial issue, nuclear testing, and a party that had withdrawn from the proceedings. But, the Court found a way around this dilemma: If French statements were found to be binding, then France had obligated itself to end its above-ground nuclear testing and Australia's and New Zealand's lawsuit was without purpose. They did not have to reach a decision in this case. As a result, the Court analyzed French public statements in order to determine whether these declarations were binding. As indicated earlier, the Court was concerned whether the statements by officials accurately reflected French intentions, their expressed consent, to stop nuclear testing (Nuclear Tests Case (Australia v. France) (Judgment) 1974, paras 34–41). The Court concluded that "France made public its intention to cease its conduct of atmospheric nuclear tests following the conclusion of the 1974 series of tests" (Nuclear Tests Case (Australia v. France) (Judgment) 1974, par 41). The Court found that French statements reflected the intention of the state.

As Koskenniemi has pointed out, the ICJ's use of intent reframed, but did not resolve, the issues that were present in unilateral acts from their inception as consent-based obligations. In the *Nuclear Tests Cases* French intentions were binding because they represented an obligation *erga omnes*—an obligation that was not directly opposable by any state. This meant that if France intended its statements, made outside the Court, to be binding, then they were regardless of the fact that they were not directed to any state. This created a universal obligation. But, this also raised the question of why these obligations should be binding on France, a question that the Court answered by introducing the idea of good faith.

Good faith created a practical problem for the doctrine. For example, if French statements were binding in good faith, then France was obligated by its word. If France broke its word, it would now be in bad faith. However, bad faith is hard to ascertain unless a second state reacts to the act, and if this second state reacts to the act the act is no longer unilateral because it is directed to someone specific, another sovereign. In addition, if an act is only binding because a state intends it to be binding, then the acting state has to be able to revoke the act whenever its intention changes. This makes sense because a sovereign state has to be able to change its intention. But revocability of an act challenges the viability of the doctrine because other states will not trust an act that can be changed at any time.

In the end of the analysis, the *Nuclear Tests Cases* was responding to the mid-twentieth century need to legalize unilateral acts by formulating these acts as obligations *erga omnes*. However, this formulation only exacerbated the problems that were evident in the earlier doctrine of unilateral acts as consent-based obligations.

Conclusion

In the years following World War II the trend was towards treating unilateral acts as autonomous acts capable of creating an obligation when there was an intention to create legal relations. This was part of an earlier movement towards "universalizing" international law. In theory, this "universalizing of law" to non-European states was based on pragmatism but in practice it only reinforced the European model of law. This expansionist trend culminated in the 1970s in the *Nuclear Tests Cases*, twin cases before the ICJ. These cases, between Australia and New Zealand and France, presented the Court with an ideal opportunity to clarify the criteria for a unilateral act. In this decision, the Court established three main requirements for a legalized unilateral act: intention, autonomy, and revocability. These newly "clarified" criteria meant that, for the first time, a unilateral act could be binding without a particular addressee—as an obligation *erga omnes*.

As a result, this chapter traced the history of an obligation *erga omnes*. This section of the chapter uncovered the core doctrinal problem with this type of obligation, the inability to distinguish whether these obligations were a procedural rule of standing or a universal principle of law as in *jus cogens*. The discussion of this point revealed that a state could not, in practice, claim standing without having had a particular relationship to the issues at hand. This highlighted a core problem with asserting that a unilateral act was an obligation *erga omnes*. If an obligation *erga omnes* was part of *jus cogens*, then in theory it created universal obligations, but there was no way, in practice, to enforce this standing without some particular connection to the act. This tension between the universal nature of the obligation, and the way obligations had to be limited to a particular sovereign translated into the series of problems with the criteria of unilateral acts that this chapter outlined in detail.

When the *Nuclear Tests Cases* decision was read closely, it became clear that the criteria established were difficult to apply at all, let alone to the wide variety of acts that are now potential sources of unilateral acts. As a result, it was hardly surprising that future decisions shied away from finding a unilateral act binding as an obligation *erga omnes*.

In sum: This chapter demonstrated that formulating unilateral acts as obligation *erga omnes* was an unsatisfactory solution to the problems presented by the earlier attempt to legalize unilateral acts through consent. Trying to resolve the ambiguity within this category of obligation by treating unilateral acts as obligations *erga omnes* did not lead to a widely applied, precisely defined, and easily institutionalized legal obligation. As the study of the follow-up cases indicated, since the *Nuclear Tests Cases* the ICJ has tread cautiously when applying this category of act as a general category of legal obligations. Additionally, the limited case law in this area indicates that there has not been a widespread appetite for applying unilateral acts in practice. The insufficient precision and institutionalization of unilateral acts, their partial legalization, led to confusion as to what exactly is a unilateral act and what is not. The category of unilateral acts was defined so broadly—it applied to any act a state undertook without reference to another state—that it became difficult to define.

Thus, in the *Nuclear Tests Cases*, the ICJ displayed the mid-twentieth century pragmatism outlined at the start of this chapter. However, in its attempt to arrive at a practical solution to the case before it, one that also effectively served the Court's universal mandate, it created new conceptual difficulties for the category of unilateral acts. This led to overlap with the category of estoppel, a principle of law that has held that acts are binding when there has been detrimental reliance. The relationship between unilateral acts and estoppels is the subject of the next chapter.

4 Unilateral Acts as Estoppels

As was noted in the last chapter, the 1970s marked a confluence of events that affected the broader histories of international law. As David Kennedy noted, as the post-World War II generation of American and European international law scholars began to give way to a new generation of scholarship,

> the elaborate edifice they had honored was succumbing to the erosion and fragmentation they had encouraged. Attacked from the left and the right, theoretically weak, jurisprudentially behind the times, the old edifice they had lovingly sheltered seemed so hopelessly ill equipped to the broad functions they had encouraged us to think it might perform.
> (Kennedy 1988–1989, 5)

The post-war pragmatism had succeeded in maintaining the profession of international law in the face of the post-World War II challenges to its authority, but it had lost its way. The Cold War between the Soviet Union and the United States, and the decolonization movement meant the universalism of international law promoted after World War II could not be easily sustained.

As Reisman has explained, the Cold War was perpetuated by "two mutually incompatible ideologies" with separate world views and therefore, international law. Nuclear weapons, as we saw in the last chapter, created a new calculus, which he called a "balance of terror" so that even core tenets of international law such as *pacta sunt servanda* and good faith were sorely tested by the lack of trust of both sides, as evident in the arms control treaties (Reisman 1990, 859–860). Further, institutions such as the United Nations, and particularly the Security Council, were often severely hampered by the veto of the five permanent members (including, of course the United States and the Soviet Union), so that the post-World War II peace and security infrastructure could not prevent the covert and overt uses of force that made up the Cold War (Reisman 1990, 860–861; Glennon 1999, 2). Further, it was in no way designed to respond to the two major challenges to peace and security that characterized the second half of the twentieth century—intra-state conflict and terrorism (Glennon 1999, 3), both of which thrive on support by outside actors, whether states or individuals, and both of which are tied to self-determination and so are either characterized as rebellions or security concerns (depending on which side of the conflict you are on).

The challenge the Cold War posed to both the doctrine and functioning of international law was directly related to the decolonization of international law. As Kennedy has explained, "By 1970, it was just no longer possible to speak of an American inspired world democracy, or to view decolonization as an administrative matter of peaceful adjustment". (Kennedy 1988–1989, 6). Pahuja has described this tension as tied international law's potential to be both emancipatory, as it supported decolonization, and regulatory, since the only way to be "emancipated" was through the regulated form the nation state (Pahuja 2011, 46). Further, she argues that the language of development mediated this tension (Pahuja 2011, 45–46). As she explains, the only possibility for newly independent states to join the international community was by agreeing to specific forms of economic development.

As Rajgopal notes, most international lawyers, in the 1940s and 1950s, both within and outside decolonizing states, adopted the emancipatory program of law as a way to build their newly independent nation states (Rajgopal 2003, 27). However, the initial hope in the newly decolonized states of the 1950s and 1960s was that they would become full partners in the international project. However, this was dashed by the 1970s as a result of the confines of international law (and its institutions), a fact which became painfully evident when they tried to implement the new international economic order in the 1970s (Rajgopal 2003, 12).

It is in this context that the ICJ's 1974 decisions in the *Nuclear Tests Cases* took place. These decisions marked the unprecedented expansion of the category of unilateral acts to include acts without a specific addressee, acts *erga omnes.* This formulation treated unilateral acts as legal obligations when the acting state expressed an intention to be bound by their act. But, this response, so emblematic of the impulse to universalization noted above, turned out to be only a partial attempt at legalization. The criteria for unilateral acts that the court developed, intention, autonomy, and revocation, did not fully institutionalize these acts, reacting to debate within the doctrine. Universalization had its limits as had consent before it.

A close reading of the *Nuclear Tests Cases* revealed how imprecise the ICJ's criteria were. Some authors even went so far as to argue that the *Nuclear Tests Cases* decision did not in fact create an autonomous category of legal obligations called unilateral acts (Rubin 1977, 3–7). A consequence of this confusion was that, throughout the late twentieth century and into the early twenty-first century, it became an open question whether unilateral acts were an autonomous act or a form of estoppel.1 Estoppel is a principle of international law that says that an acting state is bound by its word when another

1 As MacGibbon noted,

> It may, however, be argued that international practice, if not international jurisprudence, has accorded less tentative recognition to the principle of consistency; and one writer has advanced a view of the binding character of unilateral acts and declarations which appears to comprehend the principle of estoppel as part of customary international law.

state relies to its detriment on an act (MacGibbon 1958, 469; Shaw 2008, 516). In other words, estoppels promote "the requirement that a State ought to be consistent in its attitude to a given factual or legal situation" (MacGibbon 1958, 468).

Estoppels

International estoppels are derived from municipal law principles that are then adapted to the circumstances of international law. In municipal systems estoppels are justified by the need for evidentiary consistency. The same is true of international estoppels, where this need is supported by a requirement of good faith that is designed to ensure stable international relations. In other words, in international law estoppels have been justified by the fact that a state cannot "blow hot and cold," a state cannot go back on its word (O'Connor 1991, 391; Wagner 1986, 1779).[2] This wide formulation is interpreted as a reflection of a broad principle of law, making estoppels a general principle of international law (Lauterpacht 1927, 203; Wagner 1986, 1778).[3]

To be considered an estoppel in international law, an act had to meet three requirements,

> First the statement creating the estoppel must be clear and unambiguous; second the statement must be voluntary, unconditional and authorized; and finally there must be good faith reliance upon the representation of one party by the other party either to the detriment of the other party or to the advantage of the party making the representation.
>
> (Wagner 1986, 1779–1780)

The requirements of clarity and good faith had particular resonance with unilateral acts. Clarity has often been analogized to the requirement of intention that was discussed in Chapter 3. But, more critically, estoppels and unilateral acts have been justified by the requirement for good faith in international relations.

As the last chapter demonstrated, good faith required a state to keep its unilateral acts. In practice, this translated into the need for another state to react to a unilateral act before it becomes binding. This need for a reaction, however, had the same effect as the "good faith reliance" required of an estoppel. This overlap has made it hard to differentiate between unilateral acts and estoppels.

MacGibbon was referring to Schwarzenberger. He then went on to note that the *Eastern Greenland Case* (discussed in previous chapters) was effectively a case of estoppel (MacGibbon 1958, pp. 469–470)

2 Lord McNair (1924) BYIL 5, as quoted in (MacGibbon 1958, p. 468).

3 MacGibbon questioned whether estoppels were in fact general principles of law since international estoppels were less technical than in domestic law. See (MacGibbon 1958, 512).

This overlap likely emerged because estoppels were less fully developed at the international level than in the municipal legal systems from which they are derived. At the municipal level estoppels developed as a procedural barrier to bringing a claim. They are a rule of evidence that stops a party from initiating a lawsuit when it could be proven that they had had previously taken an opposite position and another party to the lawsuit had relied on that position. But, at the international level estoppels were treated as both a "substantive device" and a procedural advice in international law (Brown 1995–1996, 370, 403–404; MacGibbon 1958, 468–469).[4] So, estoppels in international law can act as both the basis of a claim and as a procedural bar to bringing a claim before an international court.

As a result of this dual role, the case law on estoppels has fallen into two categories. In the first line of cases estoppels are the basis of a claim. In these cases, estoppels prevent a party from pursuing a claim before the Court. This line of cases mostly arises in boundary delimitation cases where good faith is often raised as a basis for the lawsuit. This type of claim is often referred to as an estoppel or acquiescence. In the second line of cases estoppel acts as a barrier to continuing litigation before the ICJ. These are primarily evidentiary claims that the representations made by a party in the past now prevent them from bringing the lawsuit. This second line of cases has often emerged in preliminary arguments before the ICJ.

Substantive Estoppel

One of the earliest cases of estoppel at the ICJ was the *Fisheries Case*, which was a contest between Norway and the United Kingdom over maritime boundaries. The Court held that the United Kingdom had not protested Norway's delimitation of the boundary for a long period of time, and the time delay between the event and the protest stopped the United Kingdom from bringing their claim to the Court (Fisheries Case (United Kingdom v. Norway) 1951; Wagner 1986, 1785).[5] They felt the United Kingdom could not, in good faith, start a claim since it had stayed silent for a long time and Norway had relied on this silence in determining the maritime boundary. Effectively, Great Britain was estopped from bringing its claim even though the ICJ did not use this term directly.

A related case was the *Case Concerning the Temple of Preah Vihear*. In this case Cambodia and Thailand both claimed sovereignty over an ancient temple, Preah Vihear. The conflict over the temple began in 1904–1908 with boundary settlements between the colonial power in Cambodia, France, and

4 This point is *contra*, in part, (Lauterpacht 1927, 203 ff).

5 For a well-recognized summary of the estoppel jurisprudence up to and including this case, please see Bowett (1957).

Thailand (then Siam). France and Siam signed a treaty in 1904 that established the border between the two countries, but it did not deal with the Temple area. The unresolved boundary issues led to the signing of another boundary treaty in 1907, which established a Mixed Commission of representatives of both parties to resolve any disputes under the treaty (a similar commission had been established under the 1904 Treaty). This second Commission did not intend to deal with the region of the Temple either. But, it did join up the boundary surrounding the Temple with an existing eastern boundary. It was not clear how this eastern boundary was established and so the ICJ assumed it had been agreed upon. More importantly, as part of this delimitation exercise maps needed to be published, and so, the Government of Thailand allowed France to prepare these maps. Eleven maps in total were drawn up and delivered to the Thai Government. Central to the dispute was the fact that one of these maps placed Preah Vihear on the Cambodian side of the boundary. As a result, Cambodia claimed sovereignty over the temple. In response the Thai government argued either that the map was not the result of the work of the Mixed Commission or that the work of the Mixed Commission violated the earlier treaty and, finally, that the Mixed Commission had finished work before the maps were published. In summary, Thailand claimed the map was made in error (Case Concerning the Temple of Preah Vihear (Merits) 1962, 15, 16, 17–19, 20–21).

The Court accepted Thailand's argument that this map was not legally binding, holding that it was within the power of each Government to approve the maps and the maps themselves did not create a legal obligation. But, the flipside of this was that if the boundaries on the maps were not protested, this was the same as acquiescing to the boundary. In this way Thailand's silence may have created the expectation that the boundary was legal. The ICJ held that this could occur even if the maps resulted from inaccurate work by the Mixed Commission or that the Commission had changed a treaty obligation. Thailand's silence could be, legally, the same as accepting the maps and the obligations they contained (Case Concerning the Temple of Preah Vihear (Merits) 1962, 21–22).

This led the Court to consider whether in fact Thailand's silence about the maps was acquiescence to the boundaries in the maps. The Court considered the fact that the exchange of the maps was formal and that multiple copies of the maps were distributed (Case Concerning the Temple of Preah Vihear (Merits) 1962, 23). The Court also accepted that Thailand had not rejected the maps (Case Concerning the Temple of Preah Vihear (Merits) 1962, 24). This led the Court to conclude that:

> [e]ven if there were any doubt as to Siam's acceptance of the map in 1908 and hence of the frontier indicated thereon, the Court would consider, in light of the subsequent course of events that Thailand is precluded by her conduct from asserting that she did not accept it. She has, for fifty years

> enjoyed such benefits as the Treaty of 1904 conferred on her, if only the benefit of a stable frontier.
>
> (Case Concerning the Temple of Preah Vihear (Merits) 1962, 32)

In his separate opinion Judge Alfaro agreed with the majority judgment. In accepting the majority's decision, he referred explicitly to estoppels and he noted that "a state must not be permitted to benefit by its own inconsistency," and that more substantively, estoppel was a principle of good faith. Unlike Judge Alfaro, Judge Fitzmaurice agreed with the "operative portion" of the judgment. However, he also discussed the issue of estoppel and its relation to acquiescence and, as a result, he asserted that the defining characteristic of an estoppel was reliance on the act or a benefit secured by the acting party. This required from the parties "a change or alteration in the relative positions" (Case Concerning the Temple of Preah Vihear (Merits) 1962, 40–42, 52, 62–64). But, more importantly, to Judge Fitzmaurice, estoppels were a substantive principle premised on the good faith of the parties, and good faith had to be protected where one party had changed their position because they had relied on the representation or act of the other party.

Not all the judges agreed that this was a case of acquiescence and estoppel. In contrast to his colleagues, Judge Koo argued that preclusion did not apply to this situation. Judge Koo asserted that Thailand never accepted the map in question and that Thailand's silence was offset by its attempt to actually exercise sovereignty in the area. To Judge Koo, there was no evidence that France had relied on Thailand's silence (Case Concerning the Temple of Preah Vihear (Merits) 1962, 97).

Judge Spender also rejected the approach of the ICJ. He argued that Thailand's silence had to be weighed against all other "relevant evidence." He found that the evidence did not support a conclusion that Thailand's silence was binding. On top of this Judge Spender denied that acquiescence was a substantive principle of international law. And, importantly, he denied that an estoppel was a unilateral act (Case Concerning the Temple of Preah Vihear (Merits) 1962, 132–133, 143).

Judge Spender adopted a narrow view of estoppel. He argued that estoppel was a question of fact that prevented a party taking a position that was opposed to its earlier representations if another state relied on this representation and was harmed by this change of position. His position was that, given the facts of this case, an estoppel was not established. Judge Spender felt that Thailand did not receive a benefit from its silence and, like Judge Koo, he felt that France did not rely on Thailand's silence (Case Concerning the Temple of Preah Vihear (Merits) 1962, 132–133, 144–145).

There was a clear disagreement among the judges about the scope of an estoppel and this led to disagreement over whether the facts of this case indicated an estoppel. Because of the range of judgments, the most that can be concluded is that the majority of judges in the *Temple of Preah Vihear case* accepted the idea that estoppels were a substantive principle of international law. In sum: This decision stood for the fact that reliance created a legal obligation.[6]

The Court revisited the concept of estoppel in the *North Sea Continental Shelf Case*, 1969. In this case Denmark and the Netherlands claimed that the Federal Republic of Germany had, through its past conduct, become bound by a convention regarding their shared continental shelf. In their arguments Denmark and the Netherlands cited German actions and public statements that led them to believe that Germany was required to adhere to the convention. The Court held that this was effectively an argument for an estoppel, meaning that the Federal Republic of Germany's past conduct would have had to indicate they accepted the Convention and Denmark and the Netherlands had changed their position relative to the convention, or were harmed in some way, as the result (North Sea Continental Shelf Case (Denmark v. Federal Republic of Germany/Netherland v. Federal Republic of Germany) 1969, paras 27, 30).

After reviewing the case, the Court felt that there was no conclusive evidence that Germany had accepted the obligation. This led the ICJ to decide that, based on the facts, that there was no estoppel. And even further, the Court stressed that finding estoppel on these facts would create doctrinal "dangers." (North Sea Continental Shelf Case (Denmark v. Federal Republic of Germany/Netherland v. Federal Republic of Germany) 1969, paras 30–33). In this case Court did not undermine the possibility of substantive estoppels, but it also did not find an estoppel here.

Estoppels were discussed next in the *Gulf of Maine Case*. In this case Canada argued that the United States had "acquiesced" to the use of a median to establish the maritime boundaries in the Gulf of Maine and that, as a result, they were estopped from going back on this median line. Canada acknowledged that the doctrine of estoppel was not clearly developed and so it argued that it was not established law that estoppels required detrimental reliance. Canada then suggested that estoppels could be derived from the non-action of the other party, the traditional definition of acquiescence. The Court agreed

6 This case was the subject of a request for interpretation (Request for Interpretation of the Judgment of 15 June 1962 in the Case of the Temple of Preah Vihear (Cambodia v. Thailand) [Application Instituting Proceedings]). The Court has released its decision on the Merits of this request. In this decision, the Court dealt with the disagreement between the parties over whether the 1962 judgment decided the boundary between them, and therefore sovereignty over the temple or just sovereignty over the temple. The Court determined that the original judgment granted sovereignty to Cambodia and therefore, Thailand was obligated to withdraw from the whole area (Case Concerning the Temple of Preah Vihear (Cambodia v. Thailand) (Cambodia v. Thailand) [Judgment] (November 11, 2013)).

and held that it was "able to take the two concepts [estoppels and acquiescence] into consideration as different aspects of one and the same institution" (Case Concerning Delimitation of the Maritime Boundary in the Gulf of Maine Area (Canada v. United States of America) 1984, paras 128–130).

The dispute began in 1964 when Canada started to issue permits for "exploitation" of the hydrocarbons in its waters. Canada claimed that the United States was aware of these permits but the United States denied that these permits were "common knowledge." What is known is that in April 1965 the Bureau of Land Management of the US Department of the Interior wrote to the Canadian Department of Northern Affairs and National Resources asking about the location of two of the permits. The Canadian Government replied with the requested information leading to further correspondence. In this correspondence, American representatives inquired about the Canadian position on the median line between Canada and the United States. Canadian representatives replied that they were using the median lines established by Article 6 of the *Geneva Convention on the Continental Shelf.*

This position led to further diplomatic correspondence. For example, in a 1966 letter the Canadian Under-Secretary of State for External Affairs mentioned the accepted median line. The United States made no mention of the use of this line until 1969. Further, the United States asserted in response that the 1965 correspondence was written by officials without the authority to bind the government (Case Concerning Delimitation of the Maritime Boundary in the Gulf of Maine Area (Canada v. United Staets of America) 1984, par 133). As a result, it was said that these claims could not create an estoppel/acquiescence.

Additionally, the United States claimed that the 1969 correspondence only referred to the fact that the median line was in question. They argued that Canada never officially publicized its claim, and the Government should not have had to infer a claim. Canada argued in return that the United States had never challenged the status quo until 1970. The United States responded that the Canadian challenge to the median line was insignificant as the permits were minor (Case Concerning Delimitation of the Maritime Boundary in the Gulf of Maine Area (Canada v. United Staets of America) 1984, par 136).

The Court eventually sided with the United States, finding that they had not acquiesced to the median line. The Court also determined that the technical correspondence was not authorized, as the author had not realized the implications of his letter. As a result, this letter was not binding on the Government of the United States. Further, the United States' silence was not tantamount to acquiescence. Also, the Court denied the significance of the United States having issued its own permits, holding that this was not evidence of acquiescence (Case Concerning Delimitation of the Maritime Boundary in the Gulf of Maine Area (Canada v. United Staets of America) 1984, par 141).

The Court did give weight to the diplomatic correspondence between Canada and the United States. A 1966 letter in which Canada stated its preference for the median line especially concerned the ICJ. The Court felt that it was fair for Canada to have anticipated a response to this letter from the United States before 1969, and the United States did not make efforts to keep Canada up to date on its own policy developments, although this delay was not enough to amount to estoppel (Case Concerning Delimitation of the Maritime Boundary in the Gulf of Maine Area (Canada v. United Staets of America) 1984, par 142). Based on this analysis, the Court reviewed the case law on estoppel and acquiescence presented by Canada but held that on the facts the United States had not acquiesced to the median. There was no estoppel here, but the Court did affirm the possibility of estoppels based on reliance.

Taken as a whole, the ICJ has consistently stated that estoppels are a substantive principle of international law.[7] But, in practice, the Court has been reluctant to accept that estoppels create a legal obligation.

Estoppels as a Bar to Proceeding before the ICJ

Through the 1960s the ICJ was reluctant to embrace estoppels as a bar to jurisdiction. For example, in 1964 the Court rejected this possibility in the preliminary proceedings of the *Barcelona Traction Case.* Here the ICJ refused to consider Spain's argument that Belgium had withdrawn a similar case from the Court in 1961 and by discontinuing this claim Belgium was estopped from asking the court to hear this dispute. Spain also argued that they had been "misled" by Belgium about the seriousness of the discontinuance. The Court did not accept this argument and held that the Belgian statements could not have induced Spanish reliance to the point that Spain was negatively affected by the discontinuance. In fact, the Court reasoned that the opposite occurred, that the discontinuance promoted out of Court negotiations and these new submissions likely resulted from those negotiations. As a result the Court found that Spanish reliance did not reach the level of an estoppel (Case Concerning the Barcelona Traction, Light and Power Company Limited (Belgium v. Spain) [Preliminary Objections] 1964, 2,4).

The Court's reluctance to use estoppel as a bar to jurisdiction has continued until today. For example, in 1990 the ICJ denied Nicaragua's claim of equitable estoppel, in *Case Concerning the Land, Island and Maritime Frontier Dispute.* In this case Nicaragua applied to intervene in a dispute between El Salvador and Honduras on the grounds that the dispute affected Nicaraguan interests. The Court interpreted this claim as a request for equitable estoppel

7 Recently, estoppel has also been mentioned at the ICJ in the oral arguments phase of the Request for Interpretation of the decision in the Temple of Preah Vihear. See (Public Sitting Held on Tuesday 31 May, 2011, at 10 am, at the Peace Palace, President Owada Presiding in the Request for Interpretation of the Judgment of 15 June 1962 in the Case Concerning the Temple of Preah Vihear (Cambodia v. Thailand) (Cambodia v. Thailand)). The decision in the Temple of Preah Vihear was also discussed in the written arguments of Austria in (Accordance with International Law of the Unilateral Declaration of Independence in Respect of Kosovo (Request for Advisory Opinion)).

or recognition, deciding that this request was unwarranted because Nicaragua had not provided evidence that they had met the requirements for an estoppel. The Court viewed estoppels as "a statement or representation made by one party to another and reliance upon it by that other party to his detriment or to the advantage of the party making it" (Case Concerning the Land, Island and Maritime Frontier Dispute (El Salvador v. Honduras) [Request by Nicaragua to Intervene] 1990, par 63). The Court saw no evidence that representations had been made or that reliance was present in this case (Case Concerning the Land, Island and Maritime Frontier Dispute (El Salvador v. Honduras) [Request by Nicaragua to Intervene] 1990, par 63).

Similarly, in the *Case Concerning the Land and Maritime Boundary Between Cameroon and Nigeria*, estoppel was claimed in a boundary dispute over Lake Chad. Nigeria occupied an area of the Lake and shore, arguing that Cameroon had implicitly accepted a bilateral mechanism for resolving boundary disputes and the presence of these mechanisms estopped a claim at the ICJ. In response, Cameroon argued that the bilateral mechanisms were designed to be temporary and so could not stop them from bringing a claim permanently (Case Concerning the Land and Maritime Boundaries Between Cameroon and Nigeria (Cameroon v. Nigeria) [Preliminary Objections] 1998, par 49). The Court agreed with Cameroon and accepted a traditional interpretation of estoppel when it held that Nigeria did not change its position or face prejudice from Cameroon's choice to bring a claim to the Court (Case Concerning the Land and Maritime Boundaries Between Cameroon and Nigeria (Cameroon v. Nigeria) [Preliminary Objections] 1998, par 58).

Estoppels arose again in the *Aerial Incident of 10 August 1999* when India disputed the ICJ's jurisdiction to hear a claim by Pakistan for damages against India. Specifically, India argued that the Court was estopped from hearing the case because of Indian reservations to the Statute of the ICJ that reserved jurisdiction for disputes with current or former Commonwealth states such as Pakistan. In response, Pakistan argued that this reservation was invalid because it violated various provisions of international law. And, alternatively, Pakistan argued that even if the reservation were valid, it would not be operable in this case because of Article 1 of the *Simla Accord*. In the *Simla Accord* India and Pakistan agreed to resolve their disputes by peaceful means. India counter-argued that the *Simla Accord* did not contain a compromisory clause, a clause that granted jurisdiction to the ICJ. The Court sided with Pakistan and held that the obligation in Article 1 of the *Simla Accord* was general, and so it was not affected by India's reservation to the Statute of the Court. This provided the Court with a basis for its jurisdiction and so it was not estopped from hearing this case (Aerial Incident of 10 August 1999 (Pakistan v. India) 2000, paras 29–30, 44). In this case the ICJ did not attack the general principle of estoppel, it simply refused to find an estoppel on the facts.

Another recent example of estoppel occurred in 2004 when Serbia and Montenegro challenged the legality of use of force by eight NATO countries in the former Yugoslavia by initiating separate cases at the ICJ against each country that had participated in the NATO action. One claim was against Canada, which challenged the jurisdiction of the Court by arguing that the unascertained status of Serbia and Montenegro before the Court meant that Serbia and Montenegro was estopped from continuing proceedings. The Court rejected this position and did not remove the case from the list (Case Concerning the Legality of Use of Force (Serbia and Montenegro v. Canada) [Preliminary Objections] 2004, paras 42–43).

Likewise, on 29 September 2005 the government of Costa Rica instituted proceedings against Nicaragua at the ICJ. At issue was Nicaragua's restriction of navigation rights on the San Juan River, rights that had previously been guaranteed by treaties and arbitration. Costa Rica claimed that restrictions on the river began in the 1990s and included charging fees for Costa Rican boats, stopping boats at military outposts, restricting supply ships, restricting free movement of ships, and restricting the right to stop on the banks as well as other limitations.

In contrast, Costa Rica argued that the dispute was resolved by the Treaty of Limits between Costa Rica and Nicaragua, San Jose 1858; an arbitral award of President Grover Cleveland (the Cleveland Award), United States, 22 March 1858; judgment of the Central American Court of Justice in Costa Rica v. Nicaragua, 13 September 1916; and an Agreement Supplementary to Article IV of the Pact of Amity, Washington, 9 January 1956. Costa Rica argued that these decisions and agreements guaranteed rights including navigation for commercial purposes, rights to "touch" the banks without paying dues unless agreed upon in advance, rights to navigate the river for specific official purposes such as staffing border posts, supplying posts, or protection and the right not to have the river obstructed in violation of these rights. They also argued that there was a treaty obligation on Nicaragua to abide by all agreements on the San Juan and to work together to supervise the common border. Lastly, Costa Rica asserted that the dispute was governed by general international law. Importantly, Costa Rica argued that the Court had jurisdiction on the basis of treaties between the parties, and specifically that jurisdiction of the ICJ was reiterated in the Tovar-Caldera Agreement, Alajuela, September 2002. The Tovar-Caldera Agreement was a treaty between Nicaragua and Costa Rica. In this agreement Nicaragua contracted not to withdraw from the jurisdiction of the ICJ and in exchange Costa Rica consented not to start a Court action or any other dispute resolution process for three years. Initially, Nicaragua argued that older treaties, concluded before 1901, precluded the Court's jurisdiction but eventually President Bolaños acknowledged the jurisdiction of the Court in a newspaper article where he also stated that he was certain that "Nicaragua and Costa Rica will not need to have recourse to any court" (Dispute Regarding Navigational and Related Rights (Costa Rica v. Nicaragua) [Judgment] 2009, paras 12–14; Costa Rica Brings a Case Against Nicaragua to the Court in a Dispute Concerning

Navigational and Related Rights of Costa Rica on the San Juan River (Press Release 2005/20) n.d.).[8]

President Bolaños's statement was in fact mentioned in Costa Rica's memorial as part of its arguments regarding the Court's jurisdiction. Nicaragua tried to sidestep this statement by stipulating that it accepted jurisdiction of the Court, but that this did not preclude the fact that the issues in dispute had already been decided by previous agreements (Memorial of Costa Rica, Dispute Concerning Navigational and Related Rights (Costa Rica v. Nicaragua) n.d., paras 1.1, 3.4, 5, Counter-Memorial of Nicaragua, Dispute Concerning Navigational and Related Rights (Costa Rica v. Nicaragua) n.d., paras 3,4). Nicaragua's stipulation ensured that jurisdiction was not an issue in either additional pleadings or the oral argument before the Court and it did not affect the Court's judgment on the merits. Arguably, this was because Nicaragua implied that it was bound by the statement of its President. If this was in fact the case, the legality of this statement is highly relevant to the current analysis, as Nicaragua's president was tacitly accepting the fact that its statement had provoked Costa Rica's reliance and so it created an obligation.

For the duration of the Tovar-Caldera Agreement, the legality of President Bolaños's statement was moot but it did gain legal significance when Costa Rica included it as part of its application to the ICJ.[9] Including this statement illustrated that Costa Rica had relied on Nicaragua's stipulation that they would not contest the jurisdiction of the Court (Counter-Memorial of Nicaragua, Dispute Concerning Navigational and Related Rights (Costa Rica v. Nicaragua) n.d., par 3).

It was unclear from the pleadings whether President Bolaños made his statement because Nicaragua acknowledged Costa Rica's good faith in the act, or, vice versa, whether Costa Rica relied on President Bolaños's words because he made his statement. The first would, theoretically, have made this statement a unilateral act; the latter would have made this statement an estoppel. Costa

8 C Sandoval, "The San Juan Frozen" La Prensa (27 September 2002) trans. Caroline Pardo as quoted in (Dispute Regarding Navigational and Related Rights (Costa Rica v. Nicaragua) [Judgment], 2009) at Attachment 6.

9 The Tovar-Caldera Agreement stated that:

> 3. The Government of Nicaragua undertakes to maintain, for a period of three years from today's date, the legal status existing on today's date with respect to its declaration of acceptance of the jurisdiction of the International Court of Justice. For its part, during the same period, the Government of Costa Rica will not engage in initiating any action or any international protest against Nicaragua neither before the Court nor before any other authority on any matter or protest mentioned in treaties or agreements currently in force between both countries.
> 4. Nothing in the preceding paragraphs shall be interpreted or presumed to be a renunciation or as a diminishing of rights that each party retains in accordance with treaties currently in force in the area of international law.

Tovar-Caldera Agreement, Articles 3 and 4 in (Dispute Regarding Navigational and Related Rights (Costa Rica v. Nicaragua) [Judgment], 2009), at Attachment 4.

Rica's tacit claim of good faith in President Bolaños's statement made it impossible to distinguish whether this was a unilateral act or whether it had induced the reliance required of an estoppel. Ultimately, the Court did not address this issue in its judgment, merely stating that "Nicaragua has not raised any objections to the jurisdiction of the Court to entertain the case" (Dispute Regarding Navigational and Related Rights (Costa Rica v. Nicaragua) [Judgment] 2009, par 28). So, from this line of cases, it can be concluded that the ICJ has never denied the possibility of estoppel as an evidentiary principle, although it has been reluctant to apply estoppels as a bar to proceeding before the Court.

In both its forms estoppel requires detrimental reliance, and it is a determination of fact whether this reliance has occurred. And, as both lines of cases demonstrate, in practice the ICJ has often been reluctant to find reliance from the facts before it.

Unilateral Acts and Estoppel

In theory estoppel and unilateral acts were different obligations. However, as Koskenniemi has argued, it is difficult to separate unilateral acts from acquiescence, silence, and estoppels. This overlap occurs because estoppels, acquiescence, and unilateral acts all try to explain how a state can be legally obligated by an autonomous act, undertaken in good faith. This overlap was demonstrated in the last chapter, which argued that unilateral acts were not binding unless there was good faith placed in them by other states that amounted to reliance. And on the other hand, estoppels cannot be invoked unless the state intended to induce reliance on their act. These common characteristics have led Koskenniemi to assert that estoppels and unilateral acts are two sides of the same coin (Koskenniemi n.d., 355–356). In theory, estoppels only require reliance but practically they also require intention. On the other hand, unilateral acts are, in theory, autonomous but practically they also require 'reliance'. So, while theoretically the concepts of unilateral acts and estoppels are distinct, further analysis reveals that the concepts are often indistinguishable.

This may be why the case law often does not state whether an act is an example of a unilateral act or an estoppel, and it may be why writers have been divided on the interpretation of the case law. For example, Wagner classified unilateral declarations as a form of an estoppel. Further, she cited the *Eastern Greenland Case* as an example of estoppel. Similarly, MacGibbon, writing before the *Nuclear Tests Cases*, also classified the *Eastern Greenland Case* as an example of estoppel. On the other hand, Thirlway separated the *Nuclear Tests Cases* from other cases of good faith obligations in international law, while Franck and Rubin each took the opposite approach and incorporated the *Eastern Greenland Case* in their comments on the *Nuclear Tests Cases* (Wagner 1986, 1781, 1784; MacGibbon 1958, 481; Thirlway 1990, 8ff; Franck 1975; Rubin 1977).

To put it bluntly, the discourse on estoppels has been vague. In particular cases have not identified estoppels directly or clarified its requirements with precision. This ambiguity has made it hard tell when an act is a unilateral act or when it is an estoppel, particularly when there is little practical difference between the two discourses. They are often confused, or at best, as Koskenniemi argued, treated as two sides of the same coin. However, treating unilateral acts as estoppels has not particularly advanced the discussions over legalization of unilateral acts. If anything, it has highlighted the lack of institutionalization of these acts.

Estoppels and Good Faith

The *Nuclear Tests Cases* iteration of unilateral acts was supposed to create an independent category of legal obligation. However, as the previous chapter demonstrated, this category has proved difficult to implement in practice. In this murky context was not surprising that scholars, lawyers, and jurists have all had trouble applying the criteria for unilateral acts introduced in the *Nuclear Tests Cases.*

The *Nuclear Tests Cases* used the idea of an autonomous act, one without a *quid pro quo*, in order establish a legal obligation even when there had not been any formalities or a reaction to the act by other states. It was this autonomy that was supposed to differentiate a unilateral act from an estoppel. For unilateral acts, intention alone was the source of the obligation, whether or not it was "synallagmatic," reciprocal (Thirlway 1990, 12–13). So, autonomy in unilateral acts referred to an act that created a legal obligation whether or not there was a reaction by another state (Nuclear Tests Case (Australia v. France) (Judgment) 1974, par 43).

Autonomy has been defined as the "liberty to follow one's will" and as a result autonomous unilateral acts were not supposed depend on the reaction of other states to the act and there was no need for cooperation with other states in order for the act to be considered binding (Nuclear Tests Case (Australia v. France) (Judgment) 1974, par 43). But, autonomy did not explain why a unilateral act should be binding on the state at the international level and this led the Court, in the *Nuclear Tests Cases*, to explain the need for autonomy by the requirement of good faith in the international arena. Good faith promoted cooperation between states by requiring that a state's word would be kept, ensuring that the obligations those words contained were respected.

The link between unilateral acts, autonomy, and good faith can be unpacked further. Good faith was understood as the "trust" required for international cooperation, and unilateral acts have been considered legally binding in order to protect this trust. However, as the past two chapters have demonstrated, unilateral acts could only protect this "trust" when there was a reaction to a unilateral act by a state other than the acting state. And, in particular, a state had to be able to show that it placed trust another state's unilateral act in order to argue that the act was legally binding on the acting state. And further, it could only do this by demonstrating that it has changed its position in response to the unilateral act. This made it very hard to separate unilateral acts from other obligations based on good faith, such as estoppels that were also based on good faith and evidence of a change of position.

In the *Nuclear Tests Cases* the ICJ avoided this problem because the Court had before it a concrete case in which Australia and New Zealand were reacting to French actions. As a result, the Court was able to construct an obligation from France's statements without having to explicitly consider the reaction on the part of Australia and New Zealand. This overlooked fact made it easy for the ICJ to create an obligation in which a reaction by another state was not a requirement for legality; responses to the act were in fact a precondition for the dispute to exist (Nuclear Tests Case (Australia v. France) (Judgment) 1974, par 46). If Australia and New Zealand had not taken notice of France's nuclear tests and then decided to claim damages from these tests, if they had not reacted to the act, there would have been no claim for the Court to hear. This illustrated that both a reaction to an act and trust in the act were, in practice, elements of unilateral acts.

Koskenniemi [10] has asserted that in the *Nuclear Tests Cases* the ICJ tacitly considered Australia and New Zealand's reactions to the French statements. The Court tried to make the unilateral act meet the needs of Australia and New Zealand as well as France. Or, as Franck has put it, "[i]ntentionality, as the Court said, must be the test, but intentionality cannot be determined solely by reference to the Speaker's state of mind, but must also take into account that of the listeners" (Franck 1975, 616). This was indicated by the fact that when the Court gave credence to the reactions of other states it created an obligation from a unilateral act. The element of cooperation that was in implied in the *Nuclear Tests Cases* allowed the Court to construct an obligation binding in "good faith." Practically, French obligations were determined by the good faith placed in the act by Australia and New Zealand. France's own reasons for acting, its intentions, were never determinative of their obligation. The Court, in effect, made a reaction to the act a primary consideration in the determination of a unilateral obligation.

As a result Rubin argued, against Franck, that the ICJ created an untenable, dangerous and unrealistic precedent in the *Nuclear Tests Cases.* He asserted that an obligation must be based on responses by other states. He believed that states were unlikely to accept the *Nuclear Tests Cases* decision, and its fictional basis for an obligation (Rubin 1977, 30). Similarly, Thirlway noted that in this case the Court tried to distinguish unilateral actions from obligations premised on the reaction of other states, such as estoppels. This led Thirlway to conclude that the decision created a "dangerously wide formulation" for an

10 Koskenniemi has argued that unilateral acts always lack the certainty, the objectivity to be binding. Koskenniemi has provided a basis for the argument that unilateral acts are inherently political so these ostensibly autonomous acts in fact they require an element of reliance. However, on this point this work takes an opposite approach to Koskenniemi. (Koskenniemi, nd, 345ff)

obligation. Therefore, he argued that the decision was likely to be "tempered" (Thirlway 1990, 11, 17).

Thirlway was largely correct, as the *Nuclear Tests Cases* decision was not widely implemented, and it has even been reinterpreted as an example of an estoppel. But, treating unilateral acts as estoppels also created a doctrinal problem as it made the line between unilateral acts and estoppels even less clear. The Court has not usually said whether a case is a unilateral act or an estoppel, and writers have often been divided on the interpretation of a given case.

As was noted earlier, the doctrines of estoppels and the doctrine of unilateral acts both contain requirements of intention; and, as was seen above, intention was only to be inferred from behaviours, "the act itself". The ICJ also stated that in order to determine whether intention existed, the act had to manifest itself clearly and unambiguously. As a result, Koskenniemi argued that the ICJ had to reconcile how a state's behaviour was clear and unambiguous when that same state argued before it that it had no intention to create an obligation. The Court in the instance had to determine intention based on the facts of the case, in spite of a state's own stated intention. This led the Court into some circular reasoning as the intention of the state had to be clear from the facts of the case regardless of the state's own assessment of its intentions (Koskenniemi n.d., 362–364).

Similarly, the circular nature of good faith in cases of estoppel helps explain the confusion between estoppels and unilateral acts. Estoppels and unilateral acts both rely on an autonomous act of a sovereign state. However, unilateral acts are not binding unless there is *de facto* (and *de jure*) good faith (a reaction) placed in them by other states that amounts to reliance. Conversely, estoppels are not invoked unless there is evidence that the state intended to induce this reliance. As a result, Koskenniemi argues that estoppels and unilateral acts are two sides of the same coin. Unilateral acts require trust that, in practice, is similar to reliance, the basis of estoppels. Similarly, estoppels require a formal determination of intention, the basis of a unilateral act. On the other hand, unilateral acts are theoretically autonomous but practically they required reliance. So, the doctrines of unilateral acts and estoppels are distinct but close analyses reveals these acts are almost indistinguishable.

This explains why one response to the *Nuclear Tests Cases* was to blur the differences between estoppels and unilateral acts and to treat unilateral acts as a form of estoppel. However, as this chapter has demonstrated, treating unilateral acts as estoppels has not made these acts any clearer, that is, more "legalized," than treating them as obligation *erga omnes* did. The doctrine of unilateral acts has not included precise enough criteria to reliably establish whether these acts are obligations *erga omnes* or if it was an estoppel.

Conclusion

This chapter began where the previous chapter left off: with the assertion that the 1974 decision in the *Nuclear Tests Cases* was imprecise because the criteria for unilateral acts it promoted, intention, autonomy, and revocation, were not capable of providing reliable guidance as to when these acts were legal. As a result, throughout the late twentieth and early twenty-first centuries, scholars and jurists tried to make sense of this decision.

One identifiable response to these problems was to assert, directly or by implication, that unilateral acts were a form of estoppels.[11] This version of unilateral acts promoted the idea that acts of states were binding when there was detrimental reliance on those acts by another state (Shaw 2008, 516). As a result, this chapter examined the concept of estoppels in international law and illustrated that estoppels have been considered to be both a substantive and a procedural principle that limited the acts of sovereign states when there has been detrimental reliance on these acts. Cases such as the *Temple of Preah Vihear* and the *Gulf of Maine* illustrated the use of estoppel as a substantive principle and the *Barcelona Traction, Aerial Incident Case,* and *San Juan River Case* illustrated that it has been a procedural principle of international law. The analysis of the jurisprudence indicated that good faith reliance was a core principle of both substantive and procedural estoppels.

Good faith reliance helped explain the confusion between unilateral acts and estoppels. On the one hand, unilateral acts were not, in fact, possible without reliance on the act by another state and, on the other hand, estoppels were not binding without first stemming from the autonomous act of a state. A comparison of the two concepts showed that there was almost no difference, in practice, between the two doctrines. They were, as Koskenniemi has argued, two sides of the same coin. On this basis, this chapter has suggested that treating unilateral acts as estoppels has been a consequence of the limited legalization of these acts.

The fact that scholars and jurists have retreated from obligations *erga omnes* to estoppels was a natural result of international law's drive to try to create a comprehensive category of unilateral acts of states. It was an attempt to respond to the limited institutionalization of these acts and imprecise nature of the doctrine that have made unilateral acts so difficult to apply. It has pointed to the fact that individual types of acts may create legal obligations, but it is not at all obvious that there is a legalized category of unilateral acts.

The ILC waded into this morass when it decided to add this issue on its program. The ILC's attempt to codify the circumstances in which a unilateral act is legalized is the subject of the next chapter.

11 As we noted earlier, MacGibbon stated: "It may, however, be argued that international practice, if not international jurisprudence, has accorded less tentative recognition to the principle of consistency; one writer has advanced a view of the binding character of unilateral acts and declarations which appears to understand the principle of estoppel as part of customary international law." MacGibbon was referring to Schwarzenberger. He then went on to note that the Eastern Greenland case was effectively a case of estoppel. (MacGibbon 1958, 469–470).

5 Unilateral Acts and the Progressive Development of International Law

The last chapter brought the history of unilateral acts up to the end of the twentieth century. Until this point there has been one major attempt, in the *Nuclear Tests Cases*, to define unilateral acts as a legalized obligation, as part of obligations *erga omnes* and as separate from consent-based formulations. The imprecise nature of this formulation—it could not sustain an independent category of action without some form of reaction in good faith by other states—led jurists and scholars to look for similarities between unilateral acts and other good faith obligations, particularly estoppels. The overlap between unilateral acts and estoppels has been persistent, suggesting the incomplete legalization of unilateral acts.

But, at the end of the twentieth century, when the Cold War thawed, there was a sense of optimism among international lawyers that signalled a return to the idealism that had emerged right after World War II (Neff n.d., 26). As Koskenniemi put it so quaintly:

> Then came 1989 and all the enthusiasm about a global rule of law—human rights, trade environment, criminal law, sanctions and a world police. The end of the cold war was understood—especially in Europe—as removal of obstacles on the way' of history's natural progress towards universal federation.
>
> (Koskenniemi 2007, 3)

Koskenniemi identified this drive to universalism in a particularly European, Kantian view of international law (Koskenniemi 2007, 3). But, he noted that it was also present in a particularly American strand of international relations, a strand that Marks has identified as "millenarianism" in international law (Marks 1997).

This millenarian strand of American international relations claimed that liberal democracy has been victorious in the international sphere. Writers of this school, such as Fukuyama, who argued for the "end of history," Slaughter, who favoured "liberal internationalism" and Franck, who put forward a right to democratic governance, all shared an idea of international progress that culminated in the triumph of liberal democracy over all other political systems. For some, such as Slaughter, democracy's victory correlated with the idea that democracies do not go to war with each other, the, so-called, democratic peace thesis (Burley 1992, 451ff, 459–460, 464, 476; Franck 1992). As Marks has noted, the big problem with this notion of progress towards democracy was that it involved judgments about the legitimacy of governments that conflicted with the idea of sovereign equality.[1] This was worrisome for many states because judgments about governmental legitimacy seemed to lead to a revival of the limitations on sovereignty (seen in earlier chapters) that had been a cornerstone of the colonial era.[2]

One response to this concern by scholars within these states, scholars who had been so sorely disappointed in the last chapter by the failure of the New International Economic Order, to argue in the 1980s and into the 1990s that "international law's formal autonomy and equality offered to states in the periphery, limitations that prevented post-colonial States from bringing substantive improvement to the lives of people in the Third World" (Becker Lorca 2012, 1050). Scholars of these limitations, such as Pahuja, have pointed out in a different context that the millenarianism noted above contains a paradox. International Law claims for itself universalism, and so all states must be included in international law but in order to be fully accepted in that law, states must accept the liberal democratic principles upon which the ideal state is formed. And the state was the only legally acceptable form for this process to take. Decolonization was necessary for universalization but for many states that process meant (by the late 1980s and 1990s) accepting a model of the state based on liberal democratic principles (Pahuja 2005, 461, 463). Scholars have argued that this is a new form of colonial judgment of how "civilized" a state is (see, generally, Fidler 2000).

It was the optimistic universalism with its sense of progress for international law that prevailed when that the ILC began work codifying the law on unilateral acts of states, starting in 1996. The ILC's Working Group on this topic noted that states often acted unilaterally and that the importance of these acts was increasing. They also recognized that there had been significant study of the topic and that "certainty, predictability and stability in international relations" as well as the "rule of law" required a "clear statement of the applicable law" in this area (Yearbook of the International Law Commission 1997 Vol 11 (Part Two) n.d., par 196). For these reasons the General Assembly recommended adding the topic to their agenda (Resolution Adopted by the General

1 On the problem of progress and the link to Foucault, See (Marks 1997, 459–460).

2 As Fidler put it, "With all the discussion about civilizational harmony and discord in the post- Cold War era, international lawyers should reflect on whether and how international law is being used today in civilizational relations. In this Article, I argue that we are witnessing the return of the SOC in international law. In short, States, international organizations, and nongovernmental organizations are using international law to impose a liberal, globalized, civilization on the world" (Fidler 2001, p. 138).

Assembly [On the Report of the International Law Commission on the Work of Its Forty-Eight Session, UN DOC UNGA A/Res 51/160 1997).

The ILC and Unilateral Acts

The ILC was created by the United Nation to fulfil the General Assembly's mandate of "encouraging the progressive development of international law and its codification," (Introduction n.d., The Charter of the United Nations, adopted 26 June 1945, entry into force 24 October 1945 UKTS 1946, No 67 n.d., Art 13) as set out in Article 13 of the Charter of the United Nations. To realize this mandate, the Commission has been composed of Members who served in their individual capacities. Also, once a topic was recommended for consideration, it was assigned a Special Rapporteur who was generally entrusted with preparing detailed reports for consideration by the Plenary of the Membership. The Rapporteur delineated the topic and makes proposals for its development.

The Rapporteurs also often worked with a Drafting Committee, a subcommittee of the Members that is entrusted with drafting and filling in the gaps in substance of the documents that they felt needed to be considered by the Membership. On top of this, the Commission also created Working Groups, "ad hoc" bodies of the Plenary with specific powers assigned by the larger group (Introduction n.d.). The Members, Rapporteurs, and Committees have all worked together to produce draft documents that have then been made available for UN or state approval. In other words, the ILC was a body set up for the purpose of legalizing concepts on the optimistic (and very Western) premise that international law can be a force for progress "universally."

From the start of its work on unilateral acts, the ILC was in a difficult position, as they did not even have a definition of their topic. To begin the process of outlining the scope of their work, the ILC setting up a Working Group on the topic that reported in time for the Commission's 1997 meeting (Report of the International Law Commission on the Work of its Forty-Ninth Session (1997) n.d., par 192). A main feature of the first report of this Working Group was the prominent role given to intention. Additionally, intention was one of their justifications for undertaking the codification of unilateral acts. In fact, the Working Group offered three reasons why pursuing codification would be "advisable and feasible." The first reason was:

> In their conduct in the international sphere States frequently carry out unilateral acts with the intent to produce legal effects. The significance of such unilateral acts is constantly growing as a result of the rapid political, economic and technological changes taking place in the international community at the present time and, in particular, the great advances in the means of expressing and transmitting the attitudes and conduct of States . . .
>
> (Report of the International Law Commission on the Work of its Forty-Ninth Session (1997) n.d., par 196)

Their second reason was state practice. There was sufficient state practice, academic writing, and international judgments to analyze. Their third reason was necessity, as it was felt that codification would promote "certainty, predictability and stability" in the law (Report of the International Law Commission on the Work of its Forty-Ninth Session (1997) n.d., par 196). This last justification suggested that unilateral acts did not at the time promote these conditions it was not yet fully legalized.

The Working Group accepted as a fact that states acted internationally with the intention to create legal obligations, a position that was consistent with the decision in the *Nuclear Tests Cases.* This indicated that the ILC's project of codification was determined to progressively realize the legalization of the topic of unilateral acts based on the requirements of the *Nuclear Tests Cases*, and so the elements of this decision provide a good way to structure the examination of the work of the ILC on this topic.

Intention

At its 1997 session the Commission appointed a Special Rapporteur, V. Rodriquez Cedeño (Report of the International Law Commission on the Work of its Forty-Ninth Session (1997) n.d., par 212). Rodriquez Cedeño issued his first report for the 1998 meeting of the Commission. In this first report, he considered the requirement of intention, which he defined as an expression of will that was binding whenever the acting state intended it to be binding. It was considered part of the prerogative of sovereign states to limit their actions internationally (Report of the International Law Commission on the Work of its Fiftieth Session (1998) UN DOC A/53/10, Supplement 10 n.d., par 113 ff, par 135, par 137).

Still, he was never able to clearly articulate the relationship between will and intention. As a result, Rodriguez Cedeño defined a unilateral act:

> as an autonomous expression of clear and unambiguous will, explicitly and publicly issued by a State for the purpose of creating a judicial relationship -in particular, of creating legal obligations—between itself and one or more States which did not participate in its elaboration, without it being necessary for those States to accept it or subsequently to behave in such a way as to signify such acceptance.
>
> (Report of the International Law Commission on the Work of its Fiftieth Session (1998) UN DOC A/53/10, Supplement 10 n.d., par 142)

He conflated the concept of intention with the concept of will, an imprecise formulation of the doctrine.

This lack of precision becomes evident from some basic definitions of the words will and intent. The Oxford English Dictionary defined intent as "[t]he act or fact of intending or purposing; intention, purpose (formed in the mind)" (Intent n.d.). This definition implies that intending is an internal mental state that, a definition that corresponds with the discussion of intention in Chapter 3. On the other hand, the Oxford English Dictionary offers over 20 definitions of "will." The most pertinent definition is "[t]he action of willing or choosing to do something; the movement or attitude of the mind which is directed with conscious intention to (and, normally, issues immediately in) some action, physical or mental; volition." This definition is clarified further in a sub-definition as "[i]ntention, intent, purpose, determination" (Will n.d.). Taken together, these definitions suggest that "will" requires taking action on an "intention". This explains why Rodriguez Cedeño asserts that intention has to display itself as the "will" of the state. In spite of this insight, Rodriguez Cedeño did not to delve into this distinction in any detail, preferring to treat will as directly equivalent to intention. This decision is in accord with the lack of precision in the doctrine examined in Chapters 3 and 4.

Maybe it was Rodriguez Cedeño's decision to conflate will with intent that made this definition controversial; in any event, not all of the Members of the ILC accepted his definition of a unilateral act. The 1998 Report noted that some Members supported this definition of intention while some other Members argued that a third party, such as a court, could find that a unilateral act existed, even against an acting state's expressed intentions. These Members argued that intention was not an expression of will of the state because intention could be constructed *ex post facto* by an international tribunal. To these Members, third party observers, for example the judges of an international tribunal, always assessed intention. This approach was faithful to the *Nuclear Tests Cases* where the ICJ had in fact been the arbiter of a state's intention (Report of the International Law Commission on the Work of its Fiftieth Session (1998) UN DOC A/53/10, Supplement 10 n.d., par 168).[3]

Other Members opposed Rodriguez Cedeño's definition because they did not think will and intention were the same thing. These Members were concerned that intention was difficult to determine and so it could always be interpreted against a state's wishes. Members who felt this way felt that unilateral obligations resulted from the will of the state, the manifestations of intention, regardless of the acting state's true intentions.

The debate among Members of the ILC over Rodriguez Cedeño's proposed definition illustrated an ongoing problem with intention-based obligations such as unilateral acts. Intention was a mental state that could never be known with any certainty. So, in practice, intention always required interpretation before it could produce a legal obligation. The fact that intention had to be interpreted either by the parties concerned with the act (through diplomatic correspondence or negotiation) or a third party (such as the ICJ) resulted in debates over whose interpretation of intention should be used, the act or the actual wishes of the state. These opposite interpretations created two separate yet related problems. How could a state manifest its intention?

3 See discussion of this case in Chapter 3 and as follows.

And how could a state manifest its intention to create a legal obligation? Each of these questions created problems for the definition of intention.

Once the ILC decided that legalization of this area should proceed by adopting the criteria in the *Nuclear Tests Cases*, it had to determine how a state could manifest its intention. In this regard, unilateral acts were supposed to be different from treaties and other "consent"-based sources of law. For example, in treaty law a state uses the formalities of treaty formation, such as a signature, to demonstrate its consent to the obligation the treaty contains. As a result, in treaty law, the obligation was separate from the procedure to demonstrate acceptance of that obligation. However, the doctrinal problems with this approach led the ICJ to abandon this view in the *Nuclear Tests Cases*. One consequence of the shift to treating unilateral acts as autonomous acts was that there were no longer any procedures to determine when a state has indicated an intention to accept an obligation. The only indication of the acting state's intention was the act itself.

There were differences between obligations based on intention, unilateral acts, and those obligations where intention was supported by external indications of intent, will, such as in a contract or treaty. It is true that a state that wanted to create a unilateral obligation could choose to provide separate indicators that their intention was coextensive with their actions. But, according to the *Nuclear Tests Cases*, this is not necessary for a legal obligation to result from the act. In this case, there was no evidence aside from French statements or actions (such as a formal notification) that indicated their intention to create a legal obligation as opposed to public statements of policy. And, they did not participate in the Court proceedings, so there was no first-hand evidence of their intention before the Court. So, in this case the only way to know a unilateral act's intention was through the interpretation of the act itself.

This created the need to find evidence of a state's intention, evidence of the state's will through interpretation of what a state has said or done (Koskenniemi, From Apology to Utopia: The Structure of International Legal Argument n.d., 349). Consequently, international law has been faced with a situation that is analogous with, but not identical to, *mens rea* in Anglo-American criminal law. However, unlike in criminal law, a state cannot have a "state of mind," so that it was the state's representatives who could indicate a state's intent. In both situations, it was evidence about the State's/individual's understanding of their actions that determines intention (Roach, Healy and Trotter n.d., 418). As in *mens rea*, it was assumed that actors intended the natural consequences of their actions. The difficulty for unilateral acts has been that, much like in the case of *mens rea*, it has always been a third party who determined what a state's understanding of its actions were. As has already been pointed out, this has turned out to be different than what the state's subjective understanding of those actions were. This is different than when there are independent sources of evidence of a state's will to be bound, such as a signature on a treaty. This point became key for the ILC in 1999.

In his 1999 report Rodriguez Cedeño tried again to present his will-based approach to determining intention, although most likely in response to the criticisms noted above, he clarified that intention could be determined according to the requirements of treaty law established in the *Vienna Convention on the Law of Treaties* (Rodriguez Cedeño's second report on the Unilateral Act of States (1999)). He used the Convention as a basis for his proposed draft Article, Article 6, that established that a unilateral act had to be an act of a state made by representatives who had the power to bind the state, it had to represent the will of its state, it had to be lawful, it could not contradict other legal obligations, it could not bind third parties, and it was determined by intention. But, these criteria raised many of the same issues as the consent-based approach to legalization discussed in Chapter 2. As a result, Members did not all accept the Report's characterization reliance on intention, and some Members focused on the problem of distinguishing a state's intention to act and a state's intention to create a legal obligation (Report of the International Law Commission on the Work of Fifty-First Session (1999) UN DOC A/54/10, Supplement 10 n.d., par 541).

The differences in approaches to intention became acute when Members began discussing Rodriguez Cedeño's draft Article 6, mentioned earlier. Some Members favoured going further than Rodriguez Cedeño. These members wanted to remove the reference to intention entirely and replace this with the need to determine the "unequivocal" will of the state. The use of the term "unequivocal" signalled a stronger use of the concept of the will of the state. Unfortunately, using the term unequivocal will also added a new term into the discussion, which was then subject to debate. In the end, Members' reactions to Article 6 were mixed. For example, some Members argued that the Draft relied too heavily on the *Vienna Convention on the Law of Treaties.* Other Members were concerned that the analogy to the Convention was inserting requirements for external indications of what was an internal process, the process of forming intent. The ILC's ambiguous response to Draft Article 6 led to reconstituting of a Working Group for this topic (Report of the International Law Commission on the Work of Fifty-First Session (1999) UN DOC A/54/10, Supplement 10 n.d., par 544, 553).

This new Working Group proposed its own definition of a unilateral act. A unilateral act was :

> [a] unilateral statement by a State by which such State intends to produce legal effects in its relations with one or more States or international organizations and which is notified or otherwise made known to the State or organization concerned.
>
> (Report of the International Law Commission on the Work of Fifty-First Session (1999) UN DOC A/54/10, Supplement 10 n.d., par 589)

This definition returned to the idea of intention, but, in a nod to those who had favoured the formulation based on a State's will, it also required notification. So, this definition retreated from Rodriguez Cedeño's reliance on the

Vienna Convention, but it still did not establish how to identify intention. Ultimately, the ILC did not adopt this definition either.

This led Rodriguez Cedeño to use his 2000 report to reintroduce the idea that intention was defined by the will of the state. But, intention was a "fundamental element" of unilateral acts, and was central to the determination of whether the act was legal or political. Surprisingly, he still did not differentiate between will and intention. On this shaky basis, he proposed a new draft definition that was largely a reiteration of the Working Group's proposed definition, and it read,

> For the purposes of the present articles, 'unilateral acts of a state' means an unequivocal expression of will which is formulated by a State with the intention of producing legal effects in relation to one or more other States or international organizations, and which is known to that State or international organisation.
>
> (Report of the International Law Commission on the Work of its Fifty-Second Session (2000) UN DOC A/55/10, Supplment No 10 2005, par 517, n 165)

Once again, Members' criticism of the draft Article and their scepticism about the applicability of treaty law to unilateral acts led the drafters to remove this Article (Report of the International Law Commission on the Work of its Fifty-Second Session (2000) UN DOC A/55/10, Supplment No 10 2005, paras 515–516, 520, 526,549).

The debate continued when Rodriguez Cedeño defended the analogy between unilateral acts and treaty law in his 2001 Report. He argued that treaty law provided the soundest basis for the codification of unilateral acts. Predictably, some Members remained sceptical that the treaty model could be applied to unilateral acts (Report of the International Law Commission on the Work of its Fifty-Third Session (2001) UN DOC A/56/10, supplement 10 n.d., paras 227ff, 241). And other members remained unconvinced that will was the same as intent.

At this point Rodriguez Cedeño also drafted a provision on the interpretation of unilateral acts. This draft Article was modelled on Article 31, Paragraph 1, of the *Vienna Convention on the Law of Treaties.* Article 31 stated that acts should be interpreted in good faith in light of their object and purpose. This new draft provision was considered useful, although some Members were concerned about making intention the primary method of ascertaining a unilateral act, preferring a reaction by other states as a factor in determining the act. Still other Members favoured a clear indication of a state's "real will" which they felt might be different then their expressed will. These contradictory positions outlined the core difficulty the ILC faced; intention had to be identified before it could create a legal obligation (Report of the International Law Commission on the Work of its Fifty-Third Session (2001) UN DOC A/56/10, supplement 10 n.d., paras 243, 244).

The ILC's inability to identify intention carried into the next year's ILC meetings. In 2002 the problem was that unilateral acts were a "mechanism [that] was impossible to describe in terms of a voluntary scheme in which States had the intention of creating legal effects and in which they formulated actions that then did so" (Report of the International Law Commission on the Work of its Fifty-Fourth Session (2002) UN DOC A/57/10 Supplement 10 n.d., para 335, brackets added). Tacitly, Members of the ILC were admitting that unilateral acts could never be fully legalized.

To move beyond this debate, the Working Group proposed a series of recommendations that had been reached by consensus in the Group. Of importance here, one of their recommendations defined a unilateral act as a statement "expressing the will or consent" of the state (Report of the Internaional Law Commission on the Work of its Fifty-Fifth Session (2003) UN DOC A/58/10, Supplement 10 n.d., par 306). But these recommendations did not help the Commission move forward. There was no resolution of the issue of intent in the 2004 Report of the ILC (Report of the International Law Commission on the Work of its Fifty-Sixth Session (2004) UN DOC A/59/10, Supplment 10 n.d.) and the 2005 report did not discuss this issue directly.

In 2006 the Commission had before it a new report from a third Working Group that had been constituted to facilitate progress on this topic. From this report, they developed ten Guiding Principles for Unilateral Acts. With this step, the ILC adopted "Guiding Principles" for unilateral acts (Report of the International Law Commission on the Work of its Fifty-Eight Session (2006) UN DOC A/61/10, Supplement 10 n.d., par 170). These guidelines did not create any legal obligations but were designed to be persuasive upon states. Following the ILC's lead, the ten Guiding Principles were considered at the Sixth Committee of the United Nations, where they were "taken note of" by the Committee. The guidelines were then commended for "dissemination" in the General Assembly Resolution that accompanied the Report of this committee (Resolution Adopted by the General Assembly [on the Report of the UN Sixth Committee A/61/454 n.d., Report of the International Law Commission on the Work of its Fifty-Eight Session (2006) UN DOC A/61/10, Supplement 10 n.d.).

As the Commission noted, the wide variety of unilateral acts and the "difference in legal cultures" meant that no agreement had been reached regarding whether a unilateral act required a "manifestation of will" or just intention before becoming legally binding (Report of the International Law Commission on the Work of its Fifty-Eight Session (2006) UN DOC A/61/10, Supplement 10 n.d., par 174). The disagreement over the meaning of intention and its relationship to the will of the state remained unresolved. As a result, in the Guiding Principles the ILC adopted a hybrid definition of intention. Intention was defined as:

> [D]eclarations publicly made and manifesting the will to be bound may have the effect of creating legal obligations. When the conditions for this are met, the binding character of such declarations is based on good faith;

> States concerned may then take them into consideration and rely on them; such States are entitled to require that such obligations be respected.
>
> (Report of the International Law Commission on the Work of its Fifty-Eight Session (2006) UN DOC A/61/10, Supplement 10 n.d., par 177)

This definition paid homage to various approaches to intention. First, they included the will to create a legal obligation. Will, of course, was a manifestation of a state's intention that could be interpreted by others. Second, unilateral acts were also identified with good faith in the act. This was new, but consistent with earlier decisions. Here the ILC followed *the Nuclear Tests Cases* and introduced good faith as a partner to the will of the state. The aim of good faith was to let states know that when international actors interpreted their acts as "manifesting" will then they will be bound by the act. By incorporating good faith into its guidelines, the ILC incorporated all the limitations to unilateral acts posed by estoppels, particularly the problems with using a reaction as a way of identifying a state's intention.

In the *Nuclear Tests Cases* intention was the primary requirement for a unilateral act, but the Court did not say how to determine intention (Nuclear Tests Case (Australia v. France) (Judgment) 1974, par 43). This forced the ILC to grapple with how to define intention. In this process two problems emerged. First, intention could not be determined without a manifestation of that intention to other states. Second, there had to be a way to determine when a state wanted to create a legal obligation as opposed to a desire to act in a certain way (i.e. politically). These problems led the ILC to decide that intention was only present when there was both an act of will—a manifestation of intention—and good faith—a formal indication to other states of an intention to create a legal obligation. This dual formulation, of will and good faith, ended up effectively undermining the requirement of autonomy of the unilateral act, a problem that will be discussed as follows. In the end, the ILC could not progress towards legalization, it could only produce guiding principles on unilateral acts because it never defined intention with sufficient precision to create an obligation that could be applied in practice.

Autonomy

The paradox inherent in requirement of autonomy was noted in previous chapters, and it was not resolved by the ILC's commitment to a dual formulation of intention as an act of will and intent. Using both will and intent meant that a third party, another state or a tribunal, had to react to this act before it passed from being an internal domestic act to a unilateral act with legal effect. But, the need for a reaction to an act immediately brought into question the autonomy of the unilateral act. It also made it hard to differentiate unilateral acts from other reliance based obligations such as estoppels.

Autonomy, as the *Nuclear Tests Cases* required, meant that unilateral acts did not need any "quid pro quo" on the part of another state. This created practical difficulties with applying unilateral acts as an obligations *erga omnes*, since it was not clear how an act could be identified without a reaction by other states. The ILC was not able to ignore this unresolved problem: in his introduction to his first report the Special Rapporteur for unilateral acts, Rodriguez Cedeño, observed that estoppel was a rule of international law, although it was not often the basis of a decision of the ICJ. Strangely, he determined that the doctrine of estoppels did not have a bearing on unilateral acts. He felt that the requirement of detrimental reliance had only superficial similarities to unilateral acts because it could be passive, whereas it was the positive act of will, the autonomy of the act, which made the act legal (Yearbook of the International Law Commission, Vol 2 [1998] UNGA Doc A/53/10 n.d., paras 130–131). Ironically, in his attempt to assert the differences between unilateral acts and estoppel, he ended up confusing things further by changing the criteria for unilateral acts from intention, which can be passive, to will, a problem discussed thoroughly in Chapter 4. On this basis Rodriguez Cedeño proposed excluding acts of estoppel from the study of unilateral acts. In a short analysis, he described the "analytical" differences between unilateral acts and estoppels. However, he did not provide guidance for telling the difference between the two types of acts.

Some Members of the ILC questioned Rodriguez Cedeño's decision to exclude estoppels from the study. As Mr. Lukashuk noted in debates at the ILC that :

> [o]ne minor criticism was that the report emphasized the unilateral nature of acts of States, but the legal consequences of such acts usually arose when other States reacted to them. The effect of reactions of States must therefore be duly taken into account.
>
> (Yearbook of the International Law Commission, Vol 1 [1997] UNGA Doc A/CN.L.543 n.d., p. 266, par 11)

Still other Members argued that for practical reasons estoppels should be included in the study. But, other Members agreed with the Special Rapporteur as they considered estoppels separate from the study of unilateral acts because estoppels did not require intention to create a legal obligation where unilateral acts did and, conversely, reliance was not a requirement of unilateral acts but it was a requirement of estoppels (Yearbook of the International Law Commission, Vol 2 [1998] UNGA Doc A/53/10 n.d., paras 159–160).

In the following year, Rodriguez Cedeño restated his position that estoppels were different from unilateral acts because they did not create legal "effects" (Report of the International Law Commission on the Work of Fifty-First Session (1999) UN DOC A/54/10, Supplement 10 n.d., par 509).[4] Countering

4 ILC Report 1999, par 509.

this view, the Working Group that had been constituted at the 1997 meeting requested specifically that:

> the question of estoppel and the question of silence should be examined by the Special Rapporteur, at the appropriate time, with a view to determining what rules, if any, could be formulated in this respect in the context of unilateral acts of States.
> (Report of the International Law Commission on the Work of its Fiftieth Session (1998) UN DOC A/53/10, Supplement 10 n.d., par 199).[5]

However, Members became preoccupied with discussing the draft Articles proposed by Rodriguez Cedeño and did not discuss this recommendation. In fact, the relationship between estoppels and unilateral acts was not pursued further at the ILC (Report of the International Law Commission on the Work of Fifty-First Session (1999) UN DOC A/54/10, Supplement 10 n.d.).[6]

But this was not the end of the problem. Even though they insisted that estoppels were not part of their topic of study, the ILC could not escape the basic tension between autonomy and the reactions to acts by other states. To respond to this, in its Guiding Principles, the ILC supplemented the requirement of "will of the state" with a further requirement, good faith. This requirement was introduced to help identify when the will of a state is binding; it is binding when good faith demands it. But, this raises the question of good faith to whom? The ILC never answered this question although their work implied that this referred to another state since good faith required evidence of an intention to act (will) that would lead other states to believe that an obligation has been created. And so, the ILC was found itself introducing requirements that, in practice, blurred the neat lines between unilateral acts and estoppels.

In fact, the ILC wavered between restating the doctrinal differences between unilateral acts and estoppels and acknowledging their practical similarity. The ILC effectively acknowledged that, in spite of their stated differences, unilateral acts and estoppels were often indistinguishable in practice.

Revocation

The ILC's outline for its work considered revocation, or, as the ILC called it, the duration, amendment, and termination of unilateral acts. In fact, revocation was raised early in the ILC's consideration of unilateral acts (Report of the International Law Commission on the Work of its Forty-Ninth Session (1997) n.d., par 192, 210, Report of the International Law Commission on

5 ILC Report 1998, par 10.

6 A search by the author of all of the subsequent reports of the International Law Commission for the terms "estoppel" and "reliance" yielded no results.

the Work of its Fiftieth Session (1998) UN DOC A/53/10, Supplement 10 n.d., par 183). Certain Members of the ILC felt that unilateral acts were revocable when this was always the intention of the state. And further, to limit revocation, a contrary intention on the part of the acting state had to be established. On the other side of the debate, some other Members argued that a wide-ranging right to revoke unilateral acts ensured that such acts would not have more than an "illusory" power to bind states. But this was countered by the problem that if revocation were prohibited then "States would be reluctant to ever make such promises." These Members argued that revocation must not be "unlimited" and the analogy to treaty law provided a valid way to establish these limits (Report of the International Law Commission on the Work of its Fiftieth Session (1998) UN DOC A/53/10, Supplement 10 n.d., paras 184–186).

In response to this and other doctrinal debates, the ILC Working Group on unilateral acts circulated a questionnaire to states to determine their practice of unilateral acts. Question 9 asked directly about the revocability of unilateral acts. And, problematically, but predictably, just as positions of the ILC Members varied, the reactions of states varied (Unilateral Acts of States: Replies from Governments to the Questionnaire: Report of the Secretary General [2000] UNGA Doc A/CN.4/511 n.d., 20–21). In the following year a Working Group on this topic was reconvened that raised two points about the answers to Question 9. First, they noted that only 12 states had responded to the questionnaire. Second, they observed that the states that had responded to the Questionnaire had not really provided concrete examples of state practice. As a result, they decided that the Questionnaire was inconclusive, a point that highlighted the lack of agreement over the revocability of unilateral acts (Report of the International Law Commission on the Work of its Fiftieth-Second Session (2000) UN DOC A/55/10, Supplement 10 n.d., par 621).

Rodriguez Cedeño's Sixth Report on Unilateral Acts of States considered the issue of revocation again. The focus of this report was on the specific unilateral act of recognition. In this context Rodriguez Cedeño acknowledged the debate over revocation but asserted that revocation was available when it was accounted for in the act itself (Rodriguez Cedeno n.d.b, paras 117–118).

Rodriguez Cedeño was in favour of a very limited right of revocation, but several Members of the ILC questioned the narrowness of his approach, arguing that unilateral acts should be revocable without preconditions. This point was reiterated by the Membership of the ILC (Report of the Internaional Law Commission on the Work of its Fifty-Fifth Session (2003) UN DOC A/58/10, Supplement 10 n.d., par 295; Report of the International Law Commission on the Work of its Fifty-Sixth Session (2004) UN DOC A/59/10, Supplment 10 n.d., par 228). So, Rodriguez Cedeño's approach to revocation was not universally accepted but the wider formulation of revocation favoured by the Membership of the ILC was also unsupported. Unrestricted revocation contradicted the position of the ICJ that had established limits on revocability, primarily good faith. As a result, the ILC membership was actually developing the law in this area.

In the end, the ILC's discussion revealed three different approaches to revocation. First, Rodriguez Cedeño proposed a narrow approach to revocation. Second, several Members proposed restricting revocation to the circumstances approved by the ICJ. Third, other Members put forward a wide formulation of revocation. The ILC's approach to revocation was not uniform and as a result they attempted to remedy this instability in their Guiding Principles Applicable to Unilateral Declarations of States Capable of Creating Legal Obligations. Principle 10 dealt directly with the revocability of unilateral acts. This principle stated:

> 10. A unilateral declaration that has created legal obligations for the State making the declaration cannot be revoked arbitrarily. In assessing whether such a revocation would be arbitrary, consideration should be given to
>
> (i) Any specific terms of the declaration relating to revocation;
> (ii) The extent to which those to whom the obligations are owed have relied on such obligations;
> (iii) The extent to which there has been a fundamental change in circumstances.
>
> (Report of the International Law Commission on the Work of its Fifty-Eight Session (2006) UN DOC A/61/10, Supplement 10 n.d., par 176)

Principle 10 ultimately took the middle ground; it reflected the case law of the ICJ. As the commentary to this principle observed, there was a difference between termination of a unilateral act and arbitrary withdrawal of the act. Termination would be permitted but arbitrary withdrawal would not be permitted, presumably because it violated good faith. As a result, the ILC noted, "[t]here can be no doubt that unilateral acts may be withdrawn or amended in certain specific circumstances." One of these circumstances was a fundamental change of circumstances. The ILC defined a fundamental change of circumstances in the same way as Article 62 of the *Vienna Convention on the Law of Treaties*. As well, the Commission drew up an open-ended list of criterion to take into consideration when determining whether or not a withdrawal is arbitrary (Report of the International Law Commission on the Work of its Fifty-Eight Session (2006) UN DOC A/61/10, Supplement 10 n.d., par 176). These criteria considered whether the declaration included the possibility of termination. They also took into account whether a state had placed good faith in the unilateral act.

So, taken altogether, the ILC did not undermine the basic principle that unilateral acts were capable of revocation. In fact, they just narrowed this principle in a way that was consistent with the decisions of the ICJ. Revocation was limited by arbitrariness, and arbitrariness was defined as coextensive with good faith, a formulation that guaranteed that revocation was permitted and would not be considered arbitrary if a state acted in good faith.

Interestingly, the ILC reached this conclusion by analogizing the idea of arbitrariness with arbitrariness in treaty law, but this equation is questionable. Treaty law rests on the assumption of *pacta sunt servanda*, a principle that agreements have to be kept. However, unilateral acts do not have a similar underlying principle; there is no agreement that *acta sunt servanda*, that acts must be observed. This is problematic because it means the limits on revocation set by the ILC lack historical foundations.

The ILC, Unilateral Acts, and Sovereignty and Universality

This chapter opened in 1989 when the Cold War ended, a world-changing event that led to a period of renewed optimism about the future of international law. Consequently, the topic of unilateral acts of states seemed to fit neatly into this new *zeitgeist* of optimistic universalism as it reinforced the renewed promise of the power of legalization and a progressive international law. And it was in this spirit that the ILC began work on this topic in 1996. As noted by the Working Group of the ILC, these acts were becoming increasingly significant in light of the "political, economic and technical changes" among states, so that codifying this topic was timely and would bring "certainty" to this area of law (Yearbook of the International Law Commission 1997 Vol 11 (Part Two) n.d., par 196). And so, this topic was added to the ILCs agenda (Resolution Adopted by the General Assembly [On the Report of the International Law Commission on the Work of Its Forty-Eight Session, UN DOC UNGA A/Res 51/160 1997).

Quite sensibly, the ILC began its work on this topic by setting out to define the scope and purpose of their work. However, this effort soon got bogged down on several issues that highlighted the partial legalization of unilateral acts. As was noted earlier, the *Nuclear Tests Cases* had never defined a unilateral act and while it established intention as the primary requirement for a unilateral act, it never provided a way to determine intention except in the most general terms (Nuclear Tests Case (Australia v. France) (Judgment) 1974, par 43). Because of this decision, a main part of the ILC's work was struggling over how to define intention.

The ILC faced two problems in their attempt to define intention: First, intention could not be determined without a manifestation of that intention to other states, it required an indication of will that led to a reaction by other states; and second, there had to be a way to determine when a state wanted to create a legal obligation as opposed to simply a desire to act in a certain way. As a result, the ILC eventually determined that intention was only present when there was both an act of will, a manifestation of intention, and good faith, a formal indication to other states of an intention to create a legal obligation. But, this formulation contradicted the *Nuclear Tests Cases* by including concepts the ILC had tried to remove from the discourse of unilateral acts, the use of will as an analogy to treaty law and the need to differentiate unilateral acts from estoppels. It soon became clear that the ILC's work on legalizing unilateral acts would not be more precise than that of the *Nuclear Tests Cases.*

As a result, will, which was an external a manifestation of intention, became the primary marker of a legally binding unilateral act. Then again, the ILC's use of the concept of will meant that it was not the state's actual intention that was important, but whether they manifested that will in a way that could be interpreted by other actors. The re-introduction of the requirement to manifest intention, which was common in treaty law (for example, through a signature on a document), meant that someone else, another state or a third party, could now claim to have evidence of what had previously been the state's purely internal intent. And this need for evidence through the act itself ensured that the true intention of the state could be limited by how states or a tribunal interpreted their acts. This limited the autonomy of the act in order to establish precise obligation that could be applied by all states and implicitly challenged the ICJ's formulation of the doctrine of unilateral acts.

This difficulty with autonomy, in turn, introduced the problem of revocation of an act. If it was the external manifestation of a state's intention that was binding, what happened if a state went back on its word? The ILC never discussed reliance directly as they ostensibly were excluding estoppels from their discussion. By not including estoppels, the Special Rapporteur merely perpetuated imprecision in the concept of unilateral acts. As was noted in the last chapter, estoppel was a substantive concept in international law that asserted that a state could not, in good faith, go back on its acts ("blow hot and cold") when another state had relied on this act. On the other hand, a unilateral act was a substantive principle of international law, binding in good faith, when there was a will to be bound. But, as has already been discussed, the reliance found in estoppels was difficult to separate in practice from the need for a reaction to the will of a state before an act could be governed by international law.

Similar problems emerged in the ILC's discussion of the revocation of unilateral acts. Theoretically, if a unilateral act was derived from the will of the state, then the acting state should have been able to of revoke the act when their will changed. But this directly contradicted the need for other states to know, with certainty and in advance, which obligations were binding on them and on other states. The ILC tried to navigate this inconsistency through their Guiding Principle 10. As the commentary to this principle noted, there was a difference between termination of a unilateral act and arbitrary withdrawal of the act. Arbitrary withdrawal of an act was prohibited because it violated good faith. In other words, arbitrary withdrawal undermined the certainty of unilateral acts, and so it was prohibited. On the other hand, the ILC recognized that there had to be scope for states to withdraw or change the act or it would not be unilateral at all. To balance this tension, the ILC drew up an open-ended list of criteria to take into consideration when determining whether or not a withdrawal was "arbitrary" (Report of the International Law Commission on the Work of its Fifty-Eight Session (2006) UN DOC A/61/10, Supplement 10 n.d., par 176). As well, revocation was permitted in very specific situations, such as a fundamental change of circumstances. The ILC defined a fundamental change of circumstances as having the same scope as Article 62 of the Vienna Convention on the Law of Treaties. So, the ILC did its best to navigate between the drive to universalize unilateral acts of states and the need to respect state sovereignty.

The ILC tried to codify the law regarding unilateral acts of states, and as a result it found itself dealing with many of the doctrinal problems created by the *Nuclear Tests Cases* and that cases' aftermath. But, by returning to the issues will/intent, estoppels, and revocation, the ILC did not make progress towards precise, easily applied, and institutionalized acts. They remained only partially legalized.

Conclusion

The ILC spent 10 years, from 1996 to 2006, working on the codification of the topic of unilateral acts of states and in the end, they did not make progress on many of the issues of legalization that the doctrine faced. The ILC's mandate for codification led them to rely on earlier jurisprudence and in particular analogies to treaty law. While this was an understandable, it meant that the ILC often found themselves either revisiting issues raised in earlier efforts to legalize this area, or importing rules from treaty law that raised new issues for consideration.

For example, the ILC asserted that unilateral acts were premised on the will of the acting state. While this marked a departure from the formulation of unilateral acts in the *Nuclear Tests Cases*, which was intention based, it introduced new problems such as the need to ascertain the will of the state, which the Court had purposely tried to avoid. On the other hand, the failure to discuss the relationship between good faith and estoppels meant that the ILC did not, meaningfully, consider the relationship between estoppels and unilateral acts. Lastly, the ILC's attempt to navigate the need for states to revoke their act without acting arbitrarily meant that the state's right to change its intention was limited.

So, when the ILC closed their work on the topic of unilateral acts of states in 2006, they left many elements of legalization unresolved, merely reformulating criteria that remained imprecise. Much like earlier attempts to define these acts, the ILC ended up making guidelines that glossed over the difficulties in the concept. The difficulties faced by the ILC suggest that unilateral acts are still only partially legalized; they are still imprecise and difficult to apply and, consequently, they are insufficiently institutionalized. This partial legalization suggests that there is still not a coherent sense of what unilateral acts are or when they can be used. This suggests that unilateral acts may not be capable of precise legalization, at least as a general category, and that they are perhaps more usefully considered as separate acts, each with their own requirements. This point was reiterated most recently in the declaration of independence of Kosovo.

6 Unilateral Acts, Politics, and International Law

Koskenniemi observed that international law's teleology, its explanation of its final purpose, was to bring order and progress to politics (Koskenniemi 2012, 22). As was noted in the last chapter, after the end of the Cold War, there was a distinct sense that this teleology was now coextensive with liberal notions of the state and state-building. While many scholars from the non-European/American tradition (often referred to as the global South) critiqued this approach with its Euro/American-centric visions of the state and its focus on the end of the Cold War and not on the emergence of economic liberalism through globalization (see in particular, Chimni n.d., 5ff) there were several common themes that emerged from this vision of the state. These were a need to foster "good governance" within states, a linking of this humanitarian imperative to the promotion of human rights, a preference for private property, the idea of "development" of these states, and use of force to promote these values (Chimni n.d., 16–19).

Central to this vision of the state that emerged after the end of the Cold War was a Western focus on "peacebuilding" to continue to universalize a particular vision of the state (based on good governance, human rights, and all the themes just noted). This process took place from what Paris called the Western "centre" to "peripheral" (i.e. non-Euro/American host states) in a way that has been reminiscent of the self-improvement mission of earlier colonialism; Paris identified this as more "benign" then earlier colonial experiences, but this has not been the case for populations facing these processes. What has become clear is that this interventionism was born of a sense of superiority that the Western (often called neo-liberal) model of the state is the best (and, after the Cold War, only) model (Paris 2002, 637–638). Further, these types of peacebuilding interventions have been common since 1989, taking place in "Central America, Southeast Europe, Sub-Saharan Africa, and Southeast Asia" (Paris 2002, 637) with international and regional institutions taking the lead in these "missions," together with international economic institutions (International Monetary Fund and World Bank), national development bodies such USAID, and Western-based NGOS. All participate in these operations with the aim of building democracy after the end of a conflict along the lines of "liberal political and economic principles" (Paris 2002, 639–641).

In particular, European and US representatives have helped negotiate peace treaties, provided "'expert'" advisors, imposition of specific reforms (conditionalities) for aid, or, as we shall see below in the case of Kosovo, direct performance of various "quasi-governmental" functions (Paris 2002, 643–645). It is to this example that the rest of this chapter will turn more particularly.

The Unilateral Declaration of Independence of Kosovo

Where the ICJ started its history of the Unilateral Declaration of Independence of Kosovo tells the reader about its perspective on the subject; did the Court take a narrow or broad reading of the Declaration of Independence? Did they discuss the history of the conflict in Kosovo, its causes and resolution, or did they begin with the request for an advisory opinion? The Court's choices were not neutral. Thus, a little history will serve to set the stage for this summary of the road to Kosovo's unilateral declaration of independence.

While each side to the conflict, the Albanian Kosovars and the Serbian Kosovars, has its nationalist origin story (see generally Daskalovski 2005; Rogel 2003), any narrative of the current state must begin with World War II when Kosovo was divided between the Italians, Bulgarians, and Germans (Rogel 2003, 170). After World War II, Kosovo was made a part of the new Yugoslav state, which, given the power of Serbia in the federation, continued its pre-war policies under the banner of a Communist state, albeit a fairly independent one. World War I had been a "boon" to the Serbs, when Kosovo was made part of the Kingdom of the Serbs, Croats, and Slovenes (becoming Yugoslavia from 1929) in which the Albanian population was treated differentially, with their rights limited to religious education (Rogel 2003, 170). However, after World War II, the new federal state structure for Yugoslavia created some resentment among Serbs, who felt this structure was meant to limit their power. Similarly, Kosovar Albanians were not going to be united with Albania in an Albanian nation (Rogel 2003, 170–171). Only Tito, the leader of this new Communist Federation, managed to keep things together through authoritarian rule. This was combined with real concessions to Albanian Kosovars, who had now become an "overwhelming" majority in the territories, including: establishing a Supreme Court, a constitution, and opening a University in Pristina. This was followed by a 1974 Constitutional change that made Kosovo a unit in the Yugoslav federation. When Tito died, however, things began to change. Tensions that Tito had covered over—Serbian feelings of loss of control, and Albanian chafing at real discrimination in the territory—began to emerge. Through the 1980s Serbian nationalism grew and so did a new leader out of the former communist leadership, Slobodan Milosovic. In 1988, he succeeded in controlling leadership in the communist parties in Kosovo and another two parts of the Federation, eventually voiding the earlier Constitution and placing these territories under Serb control. He now had authority for half of the former Yugoslav republic. This power grab corresponded with a rooting out of Kosovar leadership (Rogel 2003, 171–172). (For more detail on Kosovo particularly, see Daskalovski 2005, 18; Guzina 2005, 31.) Albanian nationalism began to re-emerge in response, including protest of arrests of Kosovar leadership, in and outside Kosovo. Each action led to a further Serbian crackdown. In response, the Albanian Kosovars began to set up a shadow state with shadow institutions, and Serbia assiduously ignored these developments (Rogel 2003, 173).

The rest of the parts of Federal Yugoslavia were also chafing at Serbian nationalism, and by 1990 the majority in Slovenia and Croatia each elected their first post-Communist government. Conflict was in the air, with Serbs in both Croatia and Bosnia declaring their independence. The dissolution of Yugoslavia devolved into a conflict that would continue until the Dayton accords in 1995 (Rogel 2003, 174). Through the conflict Albanian resistance remained peaceful, and the separate institutions they had built kept Kosovo largely out of the conflict. But after the Dayton Accords, where it became clear that Kosovo would become a part of a new Yugoslav state, staunch Albanian nationalists began to move towards violence (Guzina 2005, 41; Rogel 2003, 174–175).

From 1997 on the Kosovar Albanians were in violent struggle against their Serb leaders (Daskalovski 2005, 18). By 1998 the Kosovo Liberation Army, KLA, was the primary group representing the Albanian national struggle, with "guerrilla" actions. The Serbian police and Yugoslav military responded with force, in what became escalating violence. This further strengthened the KLA's position as the legitimate representatives of Albanian Kosovars. By 1999 the situation was dire, as the Rambouillet peace talks, facilitated by the United States and the EU, had failed and both the KLA and the Yugoslav/ Serb nationalists had dug in. Violence was raging and so the United States and EU decided to intervene against Serbia in support of the Kosovar Albanians through NATO. The aim was to end the violence through an NATO air offensive that lasted three months and ended when the Serbs withdrew from Kosovo in March 1999 (Guzina 2005, 41–42; Rogel 2003, 174–180).

Following the NATO intervention, the UN Security Council passed Resolution 1244 that aimed at ending the conflict by establishing an interim government for Kosovo. It demanded the withdrawal of the Former Yugoslav Military and police personnel except for an agreed number of forces, demilitarization of the KLA and other armed Albanian groups and deployment of a UN force, KFOR, to establish security and democratic interim self-government mechanisms by performing the functioning of a civilian administration. It also was designed to facilitate resolution of Kosovo's final status. On 12 June 1999, the Security Council received the Secretary General's proposals for fleshing out this administration, known as UNMIK (UN Interim Administration in Kosovo), including a Special Representative and four Deputy Special Representatives who would each coordinate a key aspect of the regime, with specific responsibilities for interim civil administration, humanitarian affairs, institution building, and reconstruction. This last role was primarily assigned to the EU, others to the UN, the United Nations High Commissioner for refugees

(UNHCR), and the Organization for Security and Cooperation in Europe (OSCE). Under this international administration, the Special Representative assumed all executive and judicial responsibilities until 2001. At this point a Constitutional Framework of Provisional Self-Government set out a framework that divided responsibilities between Provisional Institutions and the Special Representative (Accordance with International Law of the Unilateral Declaration of Independence in Respect of Kosovo (Request for Advisory Opinion) n.d., paras 58–62).

Throughout this time efforts were made to resolve the final status of the territory in Kosovo. By June 2005 the Secretary General had appointed Kai Eide, Special Representative of Norway to NATO, to review the situation in Kosovo. His report, called the Comprehensive Report, recommended to the Secretary General that a political process should be started to determine Kosovo's final status. As a result the Secretary General appointed Matti Ahtissari, a former President of Finland, as Special Envoy to undertake these negotiations. From February to September 2006 negotiations took place between Serbian and Kosovar delegations, but the parties were never close to agreement on most issues. Ahtissari submitted his proposal for final settlement, in draft form, to the parties in February 2007. In March, a last attempt at negotiations took place. Since no progress was made, the Special Representative submitted a Finalized Comprehensive Proposal for Kosovo to the Security Council. After this, the "Troika," the European Union, Russia, and the United States, held further negotiations but they too reported that no agreement could be reached between the parties on Kosovo's final status. During this time, UNMIK supervised elections for the Assembly of Kosovo, which sat for the first time in January 2008 (Accordance with International Law of the Unilateral Declaration of Independence in Respect of Kosovo (Request for Advisory Opinion) n.d., paras 64–67, 69–73).

On 17 February 2008, 109 of the 120 members of this Assembly met, without the ten representatives of the Serb Community and the one representative of the Gorani (Slavic Muslim) Community, but with the President and Prime Minister of Kosovo present. At this meeting, a declaration of independence was written, in Albanian, voted on, and signed by all members present. In response Serbia informed the Secretary General that its parliament had resolved that the declaration was a unilateral declaration of secession and could have no legal effect (Accordance with International Law of the Unilateral Declaration of Independence in Respect of Kosovo (Request for Advisory Opinion) n.d., paras 74, 76–77). As a result Serbia led a drive in the General Assembly for an advisory opinion from the ICJ on the legality of this declaration. This led the Assembly to pass Resolution 63/3, in October 2008, a request for an advisory opinion on the following question: "Is the Unilateral Declaration of Independence by the Provisional Institutions of Kosovo in accordance with International Law?" (Accordance with International Law of the Unilateral Declaration of Independence in Respect of Kosovo (Request for Advisory Opinion) n.d., par 1).

It was in this context of conflict and competing narratives, that the Advisory Opinion of the ICJ was heard. At its root, this case was about two radically different understandings of the Declaration of Independence and the Kosovar Albanian drive for autonomy and self-governance. In effect, Serb leaders saw this declaration as a denial of their territorial integrity and argued that Albanian claims could be met by the guarantee of civil freedoms and autonomy within Serbia. On the other hand, Albanian Kosovars saw this as a legitimate claim to statehood as the Declaration of Independence of Kosova (Kosovo in Albanian) represented the will of the people and anything less would be a denial of this right (Daskalovski 2005, 19–20). So, as Daskalovski noted, ultimately, "the interpretation of the legal developments exists as part of the justification of both Serbian and Albanian nationalists of the right to rule over Kosovo/a not matter which side is *actually* right as far as law is concerned" (Daskalovski 2005, 22).

In February of 2008 the General Assembly asked the ICJ to wade into this fractious environment. The Court began its decision by noting:

> When seised of a request for an advisory opinion, the Court must first consider whether it has jurisdiction to give the opinion requested and whether, should the answer be in the affirmative, there is any reason why the Court, in its discretion should decline to exercise any such jurisdiction.
>
> (Accordance with International Law of the Unilateral Declaration of Independence in Respect of Kosovo [Advisory Opinion] (22 July 2010) n.d., par 17)

While the Court was asserting its power to determine its own jurisdiction, the ICJ's assumption of this power provoked charges that it was improperly using its jurisdiction to answer a political question. How the Court responded to these claims played an important part in understanding the difficulties with legalizing unilateral acts.

To answer this question, the Court began by assessing whether it had the jurisdiction to give an advisory opinion under Article 65(1) of its statute, the specific law governing this issue. The ICJ noted that there were several criteria for giving this opinion: first, that it was requested by a UN body authorized to make the request, second, that it was asked a legal question, and third that it should be a question that came about as part of the activities of the requesting body (Accordance with International Law of the Unilateral Declaration of Independence in Respect of Kosovo [Advisory Opinion] (22 July 2010) n.d., par 18–19). In response to the first point the Court observed that the General Assembly did have the power to request advisory opinions under Article 96 of the Charter, so that the question was only whether or not the request for an opinion was within the scope of their duties.

On this issue, the Court decided that although the General Assembly was not the primary body responsible for these issues, as the Security Council was seized of the conflict, this did not automatically mean that the General Assembly could not request an advisory opinion. But, it did mean that the Court should be cautious in deciding to exercise its discretion over its own jurisdiction (Accordance with International Law of the Unilateral Declaration of Independence in Respect of Kosovo [Advisory Opinion] (22 July 2010) n.d., par 24).

The Court felt that, "in principle," it should not refuse to exercise its jurisdiction and that only "compelling reasons" should prevent it from doing so. In reaching this conclusion Court dismissed the argument that the General Assembly could request an opinion in this case. It argued that just because an issue had been identified as a threat to peace and security and was on the Agenda of the Security Council did not mean that the General Assembly did not have a legitimate interest in the matter. To bolster this position, the Court held that Article 12 of the UN Charter was not a complete bar to General Assembly action as it had held in earlier decisions that the fact that a matter was within the primary jurisdiction of the Security Council did not prevent the General Assembly from taking up the issue (Accordance with International Law of the Unilateral Declaration of Independence in Respect of Kosovo [Advisory Opinion] (22 July 2010) n.d., paras 39–42).

While the Court was forced to acknowledge that the General Assembly had not been actively discussing the issue of Kosovo prior to the resolution requesting the advisory opinion, it dismissed this objection to its jurisdiction by arguing that the purpose of an advisory opinion was to assist a UN body in their work going forward, and so the Court was limited to deciding if the body was able to make the request and not whether they were the most appropriate body. So, the fact that Kosovo's unilateral declaration of independence had not been an active agenda item, did not, in the Court's opinion, preclude the General Assembly action. And, more importantly, it was not a strong enough reason for the Court to refrain from exercising its jurisdiction. As a result, the ICJ held, by a decision of 9 votes to 5, that there was no reason it should not exercise its jurisdiction (Accordance with International Law of the Unilateral Declaration of Independence in Respect of Kosovo [Advisory Opinion] (22 July 2010) n.d., 44,48, 123).

Second, and most importantly for the present discussion, the Court had to ensure it was responding to a legal question. On this issue, the Court decided that the General Assembly had "expressly" asked whether or not the declaration was "compatible with international law," and in so doing it asked a legal question. Still, the ICJ noted that some of the submissions they had received had argued that unilateral acts were not international acts since domestic law governed it, making the declaration a political act. This was an important argument, because it raised the question of whether unilateral acts were international acts at all. But, instead of confirming the legalized nature of unilateral acts, the Court skirted this issue and said that it had only been asked about the declaration's legality under international law. It didn't consider the question further (Accordance with International Law of the Unilateral Declaration of

Independence in Respect of Kosovo [Advisory Opinion] (22 July 2010) n.d., paras 25–26).

Additionally, the ICJ observed that a question may have political implications, but this did not mean it did not have legal aspects that the Court must answer (Accordance with International Law of the Unilateral Declaration of Independence in Respect of Kosovo [Advisory Opinion] (22 July 2010) n.d., par 27). This observation raised two concerns that the Court did not address further: First, how did it determine which aspects of a question were legal and which aspects were political? Just stating that a problem had legal aspects did not provide any guidance on how to make this determination. Second, relatedly, how did the Court decide that the problem was international in scope? The Court was silent on the first question and it did not provide any information about the international interest in the final status of Kosovo as an answer to the second question. As a result of glossing over of these issues, the Court decided, unanimously, it had legal jurisdiction to give an advisory opinion (Accordance with International Law of the Unilateral Declaration of Independence in Respect of Kosovo [Advisory Opinion] (22 July 2010) n.d., paras 28, 123). In avoiding these questions, the Court did not answer whether a unilateral declaration of independence was an internal act, similar to the example in Chapter 3 of the tree that fell in the forest but did not make a sound, or an act governed by international law. As a result, the Court's analysis of jurisdiction did not state whether Kosovo's act was ever fully legalized. The Court was convinced that its opinion was warranted and so it emphasized the legal nature of the question it was asked and international implications of the act, regardless of its political impact. The particularities of how the Court reached this decision and the difficulty the Court had in justifying its decision illustrated the lack of precision in the ICJ's approach.

Once it had established its jurisdiction, the next thing the ICJ had to do was determine "the scope and meaning" of the question it was asked. This was consistent with the Court's previous decisions where the judges had interpreted the question it was asked, either because it did not really "reflect the 'legal questions really in issue'" or the question was "unclear or vague." In this case the Court found the question was clear and "narrow and specific." The Court also considered that the advisory question was framed in the negative—was the declaration in violation of international law?—and it did not ask whether the parties had a positive right to declare independence. In making these observations the Court refused to discuss whether Kosovar actors had the right to declare independence, and therefore a right to secede from Serbia. The Court did not want to address the legality of unilateral declarations of independence more generally.

This might seem like semantics but it was important for two reasons. The first reason was the precedential effect of this decision on secessionist movements outside of Kosovo and the political impact this had on the Court. Also, on top of this, it is possible that the Court was not actually able to decide whether Kosovo had positive right to secede since this right is governed, at least partially, by domestic constitutional law, and so this question might have been, theoretically, outside the jurisdiction of the Court as a non-international or political question. In sum, the Court was trying very hard not to address what it felt were the political and domestic aspects of the questions, but in taking this approach it also ended up avoiding key questions of precision and application of unilateral declarations of independence.

Importantly, judges of the ICJ were not unanimous on this point. For example, Judge Tomka, in his individual declaration, noted that the Court had "adjusted" its question in a way that predetermined the ICJ's decision (Accordance with International Law of the Declaration of Independence in Respect of Kosovo [Advisory Opinion] (22 July 2010), Declaration of Judge Tomka n.d., par 1). More forcefully, Judge Koroma was concerned that the court had not merely "adjusted" the question; it had effectively rewritten the question. Going even further than his colleague Judge Tomka, he argued that the Court's reformulation of the question actually went against the intention of the General Assembly. Judge Koroma argued that the General Assembly had wanted guidance on the legality of unilateral declarations of independence and to ascertain whether the authors of the declaration, according to the General Assembly, the Provisional Institutions of Self-Government, had the power to make the declaration. In his opinion, the ICJ's reformulated question answered neither point (Accordance with International Law of the Declaration of Independence in Respect of Kosovo [Advisory Opinion] (22 July 2010), Dissenting Opinion of Judge Koroma n.d., par 3).

Similarly, Judge Bennouna noted that the majority of judges had amended the question they were asked in a way that challenged the very "object and purpose" of the question, leading the Court to potentially lose the faith of those UN bodies that had relied on the ICJ for legal advice (Accordance with International Law of the Declaration of Independence in Respect of Kosovo [Advisory Opinion] (22 July 2010), Separate Opinion of Judge Bennouna n.d., paras 34–36). Along the same lines, Judge Sepúlveda-Amor ultimately concluded that the Court's reasoning was not "comprehensive" as they interpreted the question narrowly without considering the consequences or context of the request. In particular he argued that the Court did not discuss: the right to self-determination and remedial secession, the authority of the Security Council, the idea of territorial integrity, the relationship between this authority and self-government and how this authority could be diminished, as well as the issue of recognition. And he felt that they should have answered each of these questions (Accordance with International Law of the Declaration of Independence in Respect of Kosovo [Advisory Opinion] (22 July 2010), Separate Opinion of Judge Sepulveda Amor n.d., paras 34–35).

Lastly, Judge Yusuf was even more pointed when he wrote that the Court's interpretation of the question was such a narrow reading of the General Assembly's intention that it rendered the entire decision's substance "void." By this he meant that the General Assembly's question included a need to decide whether Kosovo's secession was valid even without Serbian consent.

Judge Yusuf's point was that, by refusing to discuss the general question of when exactly peoples have the right to declare independence, the majority of judges didn't answer the legally relevant question of when a unilateral declaration became a legal act (Accordance with International Law of the Declaration of Independence in Respect of Kosovo [Advisory Opinion] (22 July 2010), Separate Opinion of Judge Yusuf n.d., paras 2, 17).

Having defined (or redefined) its question, the Court then began its opinion on the merits of the case by deciding, first, whether the declaration was legal under general international law, and then second, whether or not the general international law was affected by the specific law of the Security Council in this area (Accordance with International Law of the Unilateral Declaration of Independence in Respect of Kosovo [Advisory Opinion] (22 July 2010) n.d., par 78).

The Court stated that under general international law there was no prohibition on declarations of independence. And, in particular, by the second half of the twentieth century, there was a legal principle of self-determination, a right to independence for any "peoples" that were not currently "self-governing territories," referring to territories under "alien" control. But they did not clarify what these terms meant. The Court instead jumped on the point that that the general practice of making declarations of independence had continued (outside the context of self-determination) and that there was no rule prohibiting these types of declarations. Importantly, they felt this was true in spite of the fact that the Security Council had condemned specific unilateral declarations, a condemnation that the ICJ rationalized as speaking to the "character" of those declarations as either actual or potential violations of international law, so that the general principal that declarations of independence were legal remained intact (Accordance with International Law of the Unilateral Declaration of Independence in Respect of Kosovo [Advisory Opinion] (22 July 2010) n.d., paras 78–79, 81). In other words, it was possible to declare independence unilaterally, but the assessment of a declaration's legality depended on how the "character" of the declaration was assessed. Assessment of the character of a declaration was inherently political and so it was supposed to be carried out at the Security Council, not by the Court.

The Court also heard submissions that unilateral declarations of independence were implicitly prevented by the principle of territorial integrity that was enshrined in Article 2, paragraph 4 of the UN Charter. The point here was that Article 2, paragraph 4 protected a state's territorial integrity and that any unilateral acts that affected this integrity were inherently illegal under international law (although theoretically one supposes they could be permitted domestically if the state wanted). The majority dismissed this argument on the basis that both the Charter, and UN General Assembly Resolution 2625, the Declaration on Friendly Relations, implied that the principle of territorial integrity was only meant to apply to relations between states (that is, one state could not threaten another state's territorial integrity) (Accordance with International Law of the Unilateral Declaration of Independence in Respect of

Kosovo [Advisory Opinion] (22 July 2010) n.d., par 80). The Court did not discuss the obvious problem with this argument, that a unilateral declaration of independence was designed to create new relations between states.

So, on the basis of these arguments, as weak as some were, the Court determined that the Kosovar unilateral declaration of independence was consistent with general international law (Accordance with International Law of the Unilateral Declaration of Independence in Respect of Kosovo [Advisory Opinion] (22 July 2010) n.d., par 84). In his dissent, Judge Koroma took issue with this conclusion and argued that international law did not confer a right of secession from a state without the consent of the state unless it was a part of decolonization. As a result, he argued that the Court's reasoning set "a very dangerous precedent," as the Court would support secessionist groups and would undermine the rule of law internationally. And, he asserted that international law favoured the protection of sovereignty and the territorial integrity of the state "over" that of self-determination (Accordance with International Law of the Declaration of Independence in Respect of Kosovo [Advisory Opinion] (22 July 2010), Dissenting Opinion of Judge Koroma n.d., paras 4,20, 21–23).

More directly applicable to unilateral acts, Judge Skotnikov felt that the Court's approach to international law was "misleading" and potentially "inflammatory" for arguing that there were no legal limits on unilateral declarations of independence. He argued that the right to declare independence was naturally limited because international law only became concerned with unilateral declarations of statehood after the declaration was made, at the point when other states recognized that new entity, and before the declaration could have legal effect (Accordance with International Law of the Declaration of Independence in Respect of Kosovo [Advisory Opinion] (22 July 2010), Dissenting Opinion of Judge Skotnikov n.d., paras 17–18). In making this statement, Judge Skotnikov was noting the obvious relationship between unilateral declarations of independence and recognition by other states, a part of the law that the ICJ avoiding discussing. By not discussing this issue, the ICJ lost its opportunity to clarify some of the imprecision in the criteria of unilateral acts.

Returning to the ICJ's interpretation of the General Assembly's question, the Court had earlier determined that the legality of the unilateral declaration of independence rested on two things, one of which was whether Resolution 1244 prohibited this act. The answer to this question turned on the fact that by the question of whether or not the Declaration of Independence was an act of the "Assembly of Kosovo." If it was, then the Court had to assume the declaration was governed by Resolution 1244 and the special legal regime that created the Assembly, but if it was not then it was not, then the Court would have before it broader options for interpretation (Accordance with International Law of the Unilateral Declaration of Independence in Respect of Kosovo [Advisory Opinion] (22 July 2010) n.d., par 102).

It was significant that the Court chose the second of the two approaches, but this required some finessing on its part. In reaching its conclusion the

Court acknowledged that the declaration was issued at a meeting at which the President of the Assembly of Kosovo, the Prime Minister, and a majority of elected members of the Assembly of Kosovo were present (without, as noted previously, the Serb and Gorani members). Further, the Constitutional Framework and the Assembly itself were both mentioned at this meeting, but the Court dismissed the importance of these facts by deciding that both the issues relating to the final status of Kosovo were still to be decided under Resolution 1244 and that negotiations to resolve the final status of Kosovo had failed.

As a result, the Court felt that the individuals issuing the declaration wanted to act outside the UN framework. The ICJ supported this observation by five pieces of evidence: First, by the fact that the declarers stated that they would uphold all of Kosovo's international obligations, contradicting Resolution 1244 which gave this power to the Special Representative of the Secretary General. Second, the text of the Declaration did not refer to an act of the Assembly of Kosovo. Third, it used inclusive language and not the "third person singular" and fourth, it used a different procedure for signature than the one that Resolution 1244 required. Fifth and finally, the Secretary General never had the declaration published in the Official Gazette. Additionally, the Majority took notice of the fact that Special Representative of the Secretary General was silent on declaration of independence, which the Court took as evidence that the Representative did not consider the declaration an act of the Assembly. For all these reasons, the Court decided this was an act of representatives of the Kosovar people, not UNMIK institutions.(Accordance with International Law of the Unilateral Declaration of Independence in Respect of Kosovo [Advisory Opinion] (22 July 2010) n.d., paras 104–109).

In contrast, Judge Yusuf considered the Court's whole line of reasoning difficult since he felt the Constitutional Framework under UNMIK created domestic, not international law (Accordance with International Law of the Declaration of Independence in Respect of Kosovo [Advisory Opinion] (22 July 2010), Separate Opinion of Judge Yusuf n.d., par 20–21). This was perhaps because, as Judge Bennouna perceptively pointed out, in order to say the declaration was an act of international law the Court had, oddly, to argue that the act was not the act of the Assembly that the UN Framework had created (Accordance with International Law of the Declaration of Independence in Respect of Kosovo [Advisory Opinion] (22 July 2010), Separate Opinion of Judge Bennouna n.d., par 46). These criticisms demonstrate the very elastic approach to interpretation required to fully legalize a unilateral act.

Once the Majority of the Court determined the Unilateral Declaration of Independence was not the act of the Assembly of Kosovo, it then had to decide whether or not this act was banned by Resolution 1244 and the special legal regime it created. To answer this question the Court looked in detail at the Resolution, focusing on the fact that, in contrast to other Resolutions, the Security Council did not set out any specifics relating to the final status of Kosovo. As a result, the ICJ determined that the Resolution was equivocal about the final status arrangements and so it did not prevent the Kosovar representatives from issuing their Unilateral Declaration of Independence. And, because the Court had already found that the representatives did not act within the UNMIK framework, they were not bound to this framework in how or when they issued this declaration and they could not "violate" this framework. As a result, the Court concluded, by a vote of 10 votes to 4 that Kosovo's unilateral declaration of independence did not violate general international law, UN Security Council Resolution 1244 or the UNMIK framework (Accordance with International Law of the Unilateral Declaration of Independence in Respect of Kosovo [Advisory Opinion] (22 July 2010) n.d., paras 100, 113–114, 118–119, 122–123).

Here again, four of the judges who did not join the Majority opinion offered strong reasoning (See particularly the opinion of Judge Canado-Trinidade, accordance with International Law of the Declaration of Independence in Respect of Kosovo [Advisory Opinion] (22 July 2010), Separate Opinion of Judge Cancado-Trinidade n.d., paras 1–2). Given the number and strength of the dissenting opinions, it seems fair to conclude that this case is opaque. It highlights why unilateral acts, such as unilateral declarations of independence, are difficult to apply in practice and are troublesome for international law to explain. These acts are only partially legalized.

Legalization and Kosovo's Unilateral Declaration of Independence

Peters, as well as Howse and Teitel, have observed that in the Kosovo case the Court was not only assessing a unilateral declaration of independence, but the legal consequences of that declaration, secession (Peters 2011, 96; Howse 2010). So, by narrowly defining the question the Court was, as several of the judges pointed out, simply ignoring the consequences of its decision.

The Court's approach was not predetermined. As Peters notes, the ICJ could have provided alternate, and more complete, answers to the questions they were asked. She argued that the Court could have banned secession, it might have created a right to secede, it might have implicitly allowed or justified secessionist claims, or it might have stayed silent on the issue, leaving a vacuum in the law (Peters 2011, 98). And, she suggests, each of these outlooks on secession was related to various assumptions the ICJ made that foreground its decision on Kosovo.

Peters called the ICJ's first assumption one of timing. She argued that secession has been considered legal or illegal depending on who asks the question and when the question is asked. Before a declaration of independence, when a legal advisor may have had to give an opinion on the legality of secession, the question was whether or not there was a right to secede; but after the fact, the judges do not have to discuss the right to secede, just whether secession is permitted in this particular case (see, for a similar perspective, although not called timing, Howse 2010, 842). The law may appear to be prescriptive, but as a matter of timing the law always enters the picture only after the fact when a declaration of independence is challenged. Peters called this the *ex ante* prescriptive nature of law. She suggested that in this case the Court was correct to ignore this *ex ante* prescriptive function because it was not asked a general question about a right to secession and would have probably been accused of judicial activism or faced division in the Court had it addressed this issue (Peters 2011, 98).

By raising the assumption of timing, Peters was pointing out that the legality of a unilateral act also requires an examination of the consequences of the unilateral act. In this case the specific issue is secession and the role other states could or should play in recognizing a unilateral declaration of independence. The Court divorced the Kosovar declaration of independence from the way other states reacted (either in recognition or non-recognition) to that act in order to avoid the wider question of the consequences of the declaration, such as secession. But in doing so it ignored the role that recognition played in a unilateral declaration of independence, as the Court determined that recognition did not impact on the legality of the declaration itself. As a consequence, the Court took an approach that was consistent with its approach to other unilateral acts, that the legality a state's unilateral action is divorced from reactions to the act. But, Peters pointed out how artificial this decision was, as it was only a result of when the Court began to assess legality of an act. This made the entire decision imprecise.

Next Peters said the Court assumed a "binarism and silence of the law" (Peters 2011, 98). She argued, in a position consistent with that of several of the judges, that just because the Kosovar declaration did not violate international law this meant it was "in accordance with" the law. In fact, this may have indicated "some disapproval" of the act. The majority did not acknowledge that there was a difference between an act being in accordance with the law and states approving of the declaration. This was because the Court was operating on the assumption that a legal act was either permitted or prohibited, a position which Peters called binarism. In the case of Kosovo, the law was silent, and whether the act was permitted or prohibited rested on how the silence was interpreted. Did silence mean the declaration was prohibited? If this was the case, then the unilateral declaration was illegal; but if this was not the case, then the unilateral declaration was permitted. Interpreting silence has often proven difficult for the law, as there is not much evidence on which to interpret why the law was silent (Peters 2011, 99). Further, the Court's refusal to discuss silence was similar to the ICJ's insistence that unilateral acts are separate from estoppels—it helped the Court to ignore the role silence played as a *de facto* reaction of other states to an act.

To explain, Peters pointed out but did not fully contextualize the problem of binarism and its relationship to silence. In the case of unilateral declarations, the problem of interpretation of silence was ultimately tied to the problem of intention-based obligations. As Judge Koroma noted is his dissent, in deciding that the Kosovar Unilateral Declaration of Independence was not prohibited by any rule of general international law, the Court was adopting an intent-based approach. An intent-based approach meant that any group wishing to secede had to only intend to declare independence for it to take effect (Accordance with International Law of the Declaration of Independence in Respect of Kosovo [Advisory Opinion] (22 July 2010), Dissenting Opinion of Judge Koroma n.d., par 5). Importantly, the Court's decision implied that this is true even when it would disrupt another principle of general international law, territorial integrity. So, building on Peters, it is arguable that one side effect of the assumption of binarism is to privilege the intention of the acting state over reactions to that act. By doing this, the Court was being consistent with its previous decision in the *Nuclear Tests Cases.* But, as has already been discussed, in reality intention cannot be determined without considering reactions to the act.

Peters said the Court's third assumption was tied to the *Lotus* judgment, which was discussed in Chapter 2, where the Permanent Court of International Justice (PCIJ) had held that whatever was not expressly prohibited to states was permitted to them as part of their right to sovereignty.[1] But, as she noted, this principle only applied to States and so the Court was right not to refer to it explicitly, especially since the ICJ was applying this principle "against" a recognized state's interest in territorial integrity. In other words, their decision was actually in direct conflict with the Lotus principle. Also, this approach was consistent with the majority's holding that the unilateral declaration of independence of Kosovo was not an act of the Kosovo Assembly, and so it was not an act of state. Still, avoiding this principle did not resolve the larger issue of the silence of the law on the question of secession, as it was not obvious that silence meant that a state was free to act. It could just imply a "law-free zone". In the Kosovo decision the Court did not take sides on this question, so it did not engage with what has been a lively debate over the meaning of silence in international law (Peters 2011, 100–101). The *Lotus* case was one prominent decision in favour of the presumption of freedom of action, but this has been disputed as overly "state centric" as a vision of international law (Howse 2010)).

In this case, the Court narrowed the question posed to it in such a way that it would not have to engage with the consequences of its decision. As judges such as Cançado-Trinidade noted, this narrowing was artificial and stripped the decision of any context. By ignoring the relationship of unilateral declarations of independence to secession, and by inventing a rule of law, based on an inverted version the *Lotus* principle, that anything not prohibited to states is permitted, the Court avoided the suggestion that there was no law covering this question, that it was purposefully engaging in legalization. But, as a result it also avoided clarifying the difference between the political act of recognizing a new state created through secession, and the legal act of declaring

1 PCIJ, *SS Lotus Case (France v. Turkey)*, PCIJ Rep (1927) Series A No. 10, 18–19 as quoted in (Peters 2011, 100).

independence. This allowed the Court to avoid any general discussion of the unilateral declaration of independence as a unilateral act. This lent credence to the conclusion that the legalization of unilateral acts has only been partial and that it would more productive to think of these acts as discrete acts that may have legal effects.

Peters drew out some additional assumptions of the *Kosovo Advisory Opinion*, but reviewing these takes the discussion away from the question of the declaration of independence as a legal unilateral act. Peters' discussion of the assumptions behind the Kosovo decision highlighted the fact that this decision did not progress towards the legalization of unilateral acts. First, Peters and Howse and Teitel noted that, by narrowing the question posed to it, the Court separated out the legality of the act from its consequences. This demonstrated the difficulty the ICJ had in differentiating between the act itself and the recognition of the act and the trouble it had defining the scope of the act. Second, the notion of binarism illustrated the difficulty the Court had in determining a state's intention to create legal obligations. Lastly, the Court's inversion of the Lotus principle meant that (much like at the ILC) the question of the role of acquiescence and the response of other states in creating a binding unilateral act remained undetermined by the Court. This meant that the Court left open three main doctrinal questions about unilateral acts that still remain to be clarified. Does the effect of the act on other states matter? Does a unilateral act require an act of "will" that can be responded to other states? And how does one determine a state's intention if not by interpreting this act itself? This decision left a role for the ICJ and other states in determining the meaning of the unilateral act, in contrast to the decision in the *Nuclear Tests Cases*. Together, these open questions illustrate the ongoing difficulties in applying unilateral acts as a legal category. These issues led the majority of judges to use a recognized solution, treating these declarations as intent-based obligations. However, this approach just perpetuated the lack of precision that surrounds these acts.

Conclusion

Issued in 2011, the Kosovo Advisory Opinion was a recent chapter in the history of unilateral acts. And, as the review of this case demonstrates, the Kosovo Advisory Opinion did not make progress towards the legalization of unilateral acts.

In its analysis of whether a unilateral declaration of independence was 'in accordance' with international law, the ICJ separated the act of declaring independence from its consequence, secession. The majority held that Kosovo's declaration of independence could be legal but its consequences, secession, were political. The effect of this was to decline to establish clear rules on secession. And, in doing this the Court lost an opportunity to make unilateral acts more precise, or at least to clarify that unilateral declarations of independence are a separate obligation international law.

In the Kosovo Advisory Opinion the Court followed the pattern first developed in the 1975 ICJ decisions in the *Nuclear Tests Cases* where intention was made a core requirement of a unilateral act. Much like in the *Nuclear Tests Cases*, the Court was faced with the problem of delineating between unilateral acts and reactions to these acts. In the *Nuclear Tests Cases* the issue was whether or not the unilateral act could be separated from other states' responses to that act, and the same question is at issue here. The ICJ considered the Unilateral Declaration of Independence be "in accordance" with international law without addressing how the consequences of this act, secession, impacted on this assessment. Much like in the *Nuclear Tests Cases*, the Court could not sustain this artificial separation.

This decision demonstrated that unilateral acts remain only partially legalized. This was why the Court found it so hard to apply the general doctrine of unilateral acts in this case, avoiding all mention of unilateral acts as a category of obligation in international law. This decision supports the argument that unilateral acts are not precise, or institutionalized enough, to be fully applied in international law. It also suggests that some specific unilateral acts, like unilateral declarations of independence, may be legal, but that the unilateral acts as a whole are only partially legalized.

7 Conclusion

> . . . the 'war against terror' is a war without end; it is a war in which states singly and in concert, violently engage a whole range of amorphous and cross-border and non-state actors and networks; a war that may remain so un-winnable on either side as to obliterate the very distinction drawing bright lines between victory and defeat.
>
> (Baxi 2005, 28)

The last chapter focused on the Kosovar Declaration of Independence, which took place in 2008 and the ICJ decision on this declaration which was rendered in 2011. In between when that chapter opened and where it closed, the liberal consensus that reigned within international law during the 1990s was sorely challenged. The events of 11 September 2001, "inaugurated a new era of international relations in so radically significant a way as to justify the retrenchment or severe weakening of certain fundamental, indeed constitutional norms of international law" (Okafor 2005, 172) and inaugurated a new form of international unilateralism, which Baxi has called, "circuits of nihilism" (Baxi 2005, 42). As Okafor noted, the arguments for this newness include the magnitude of the acts, the idea of changing world orders through acts of terror without central state actors (Okafor 2005, 181–186). This This notion of "newness" (of which Okafor and Baxi are very sceptical) has challenged post-World War II principles of international law such as the restrictions on unilateral use of force, restrictions on torture, and comity. This has been evident in justifications of international actions such as the invasion of Iraq, international action in Afghanistan, and more recently actions in Syria and against the new threat, the Islamic State, which has been operating across the Middle East region. While President Obama understood his policies as "correctives" to the Global War on Terror fostered by the previous president, George W. Bush, his heavy reliance on drone warfare meant that while the terminology changed, the actual practices of international law did not change much during his administration (Stern 2015). Further, given his purposeful attempt to revoke Obama-era multilateral policies such as the Paris Climate Accord (Thomas-Peter 2018) and his official statement of US foreign policy, the national security strategy that prioritizes "America First" through a policy of "principled realism" and aims to "lead" in multilateral fora (National Security Strategy of the United States of America (December 2017) 2017), it is very likely that some form of American unilateralism will be deepened under President Trump, provoking a reaction among other states. Thus, it is timely and important that this book opened with its discussion of the uses and misuses of the terminology around unilateralism.

This book has traced these modern readings of the term unilateral by investigating meaning of the term unilateral acts through a history of the legal doctrine of unilateral acts and the various attempts to shape that doctrine and legalize these acts. This process began in the nineteenth century, as by that time three main forms of unilateral acts had emerged: unilateral acts that had been distilled into treaty form, declarations of independence, and declarations of peace.

As was noted, the Paris Declaration on Maritime Law of 1856 exemplified the first form of unilateral act, one that was eventually formed into a written treaty. Westlake, in discussing this declaration, conceptualized it as a form of a treaty that was binding when it was written and then backed up by consent of the highest authorities of the state through their signatures. Also, common in the nineteenth century was the use of unilateral declarations of independence. This was the process by which an entity could transition from a non-sovereign entity to an independent state. This discussion of when and how an entity can become a state has continued to today, as was evident from the discussion in Chapter 6 of Kosovo and recent moves to independence in Catalonia and Iraqi Kurdistan (Zucchino 2017; Stone 2017). However, in the nineteenth century the main site of unilateral declarations of independence was Central and South America. The example the Introduction focused on was Argentina's 1816 declaration of independence from Spain. As was noted in this discussion, while unilateral acts of independence were theoretically permitted by international law, in the nineteenth century it was only when other states recognized this act that the declaration was valid. The Kosovo case indicated that it is still an open debate whether a declaration of independence has independent legal authority as a unilateral act or if, as in the nineteenth century, the "facts" that it represented, effective control and independence, were what created the state. Lastly, in the nineteenth century unilateral declarations were considered a way to end conflicts. However, as Westlake noted, it was generally preferred that conflicts should be ended by treaty. This implied that up to the twentieth century any of these other ways of ending hostilities were political or a matter of diplomatic practice until a treaty was concluded (Westlake 1910, 5).

This led me to conclusion that in the nineteenth century unilateral acts were not, generally, binding unless they were codified a treaty. This meant that they were not truly unilateral as they ultimately rested on agreement between states. And, outside of the case of codification, unilateral acts were considered political acts. In short, in the nineteenth century, unilateral acts were seen as a form of a promise, a step towards creating a positive legal obligation.

I then tracked the expansion of this category of international act from the nineteenth century into a general category of legal obligation. My aim in this book was to trace this shift historically. This narrow focus allowed me to highlight the changes in the understanding of unilateral acts over the course of the nineteenth and twentieth centuries. By limiting the discussion in this way, I was able to demonstrate that the process by which these acts came to be regarded as legal was a challenge to the bases of international law doctrines.

I have provided a history of the doctrine of these acts and, through this history I have explained why the doctrine has not been able to comprehensively "institutionalize" unilateral acts in a way that is "precise" and easily applied by a decision maker (Abbott, et al. 2000, 402). In other words, the main reason that these acts have proven difficult to delineate is that these acts do not take a form that is readily amenable to legalization. This has made it difficult to categorize these acts within international law. By the time the ILC took up this topic, from 1996–2006, the difficulties were apparent. And, as I noted, this work never produced an agreed-upon definition of a unilateral act (Report of the International Law Commission on the Work of its Fifty-Eight Session (2006) UN DOC A/61/10, Supplement 10 n.d.). The ultimate product of their work was non-binding guidelines and in these guidelines they skilfully avoided the problem of determining the form of unilateral acts. This was just one recent example of the repeated attempts to establish a legal category of unilateral acts.

One obvious weakness of this approach was that it assumed that it was easy to tell when an act was unilateral. In fact, it was not always clear when an act was unilateral. This problem was not new, as Chapter 2 discussed one the most cited examples of a unilateral act, the *Eastern Greenland Case*, which occurred in the course of negotiations and then a Court case. A core question in this case was whether the acts involved were unilateral or part of reciprocal discussions between states. A further example of this problem was the Kosovar declaration of independence that was discussed in Chapter 6. Again, the question here was, as it was in the nineteenth century, whether or not these acts were truly unilateral and context free, or part of a wider context of international action? The inability to answer this question in any given situation demonstrated that these acts have not been fully legalized into a precise, applicable, category within the doctrine of international law.

My approach to arriving at this conclusion has been unique. By focusing specifically on the history of the doctrine of unilateral acts, I have filled a gap in the academic literature on unilateral acts and I have contributed to the understanding of unilateral acts and to the debates within international law about what unilateral acts are and how they work, as well as to broader discussions about how international law is created.

My aim has been to show that the process of legalizing unilateral acts has been a challenge for international law since its origins in nineteenth-century attempts to formally regulate this area of law. I have traced these shifts in the doctrine order to show how the problems with legalization of unilateral acts are not new although they are still being faced today. Chapter 2 explored the argument that into the nineteenth century legal doctrine did not distinguish between unilateral acts that were diplomatic or political acts and unilateral acts that had legal implications. This chapter suggested that during the nineteenth century this shifted and international law began to treat these acts as legal acts so that by the start of the twentieth century these acts were sometimes considered as consent-based obligations. This chapter also identified the difficulties that consent presented for legalizing unilateral acts. The example of the Monroe Doctrine showed the weaknesses of trying to construct consent from conflicting sources of evidence, and how contorted consent had to become in order to be applied to the facts of unilateral acts. This initial form of legalization came to be seen as untenable.

Eventually the notion of consent gave way to new interpretations of these acts, culminating in the ICJ's interpretation of unilateral acts as obligations *erga omnes*, the subject of Chapter 3. This too had its limitations, as was highlighted in the discussion of the weaknesses of the ICJ's decision in the *Nuclear Tests Cases* and in the blurry doctrinal understanding of the differences between unilateral acts and estoppels, the topic of Chapter 4. These troublesome categories were highlighted once again in the ILC's work on unilateral acts, which was set out in Chapter 5. In Chapter 6 the doctrine was kept current by looking at the ICJ's Advisory Opinion on Kosovo.

What this doctrinal history has illustrated is that throughout the "modern" period of international law there have been progressive attempts to "legalize" the category of unilateral acts, creating interlocking attempts to create binding obligations from any acts states would engage in without reference to another state. These developments reached their apex in the *Nuclear Tests Cases*, when the Court did an end run around the issue of the legality of above-ground nuclear testing when it held that French public statements were sufficient to create a legally binding obligation to refrain from nuclear testing, an obligation that was both unilateral and binding *erga omnes* (as a promise made to the world at large). This decision established that unilateral acts had a general legal form based on intent of the actor, independent of any outward consent to undertake an obligation. This current articulation of the doctrine was particularly problematic from the standpoint of legalization—intention was both imprecise and very difficult to apply in practice.

This lack of precision has only led to confusion between unilateral acts estoppels, a doctrine that was designed to prevent states from playing both "hot and cold" on an issue. By examining the ICJ's decision in the case of the *Temple of Preah Vihear*, where sovereignty over a temple mount on the border between Cambodia and Thailand was at issue, it became apparent that estoppels were a different way of viewing the same acts that could be formulated unilaterally. And, the case illustrated that it was not necessarily easier to identify an estoppel than it was to identify intention. The decisions in both the *Nuclear Tests Cases* and in the *Temple of Preah Vihear* highlighted the imprecise nature of the legalization of unilateral acts, which has not made them easier to identify or apply.

These problems in the doctrine made the work of the ILC on the topic of International Law Commission on the topic of unilateral acts of states complicated. As Chapter 5 shows, the ILC's work on codification was not able to progress further towards "legalizing" unilateral acts. After 10 years of work, the guidelines they produced did not seem to resolve any of the issues raised by earlier attempt to "legalize" unilateral acts. In fact, Chapter 5 highlighted the similarities between the ILC's approach to legalization, which it was argued focused on three aspects of these acts, intention/will to create legal obligations, revocability, and estoppel, and the earlier debates within the doctrine. This overlap, while only natural given the mandate of the ILC to progressively develop international law, meant, in practice, that the ILC ended up repeating, and not advancing, the problems of legalization identified in earlier chapters. The need to construct will was very similar to the need to construct consent. The problem of using intention as the form of unilateral acts raised issues of the autonomy of unilateral acts and their relationship to non-reciprocal legal obligations such as estoppels. This led to questions of how one could change or revoke unilateral acts. These basic problems were left unresolved by the ILC, meaning the form of unilateral act is still ill defined. This has made the work of the ILC very hard to apply to actual acts of states. In fact, the subject of Chapter 6, the recent advisory opinion of the ICJ on Kosovar independence, barely mentioned this work, treating unilateral declarations of independence as a unique category of international law.

In fact, it is this final chapter that has highlighted the main argument of this book, that the various attempts to institutionalize, make precise, and apply a general category of unilateral acts within the doctrine has failed. While there is widespread agreement that unilateral acts are a category within the doctrine, there has been no similar agreement on the form these acts should take. This has resulted in various statements of the doctrine that are unclear and difficult to apply in practice. In fact, this doctrinal history has shown how naïve it would be for me to suggest that the category of unilateral acts is more precisely defined now than in the nineteenth century when only three types of unilateral acts were considered to have legal effect. Since that time, I would argue that specific types of unilateral acts have received more attention within the doctrine with their own disparate paths to legalization. Examples that come to mind include reservations to treaties, promises, and notifications. These acts may well deserve to be recognized as legally binding acts within the doctrine as they are more precisely defined if not more easily applied. But it has not been my purpose to trace these individual histories. Instead, I have systematically traced the doctrine of unilateral acts, as a category, and shown how weakly these acts have been legalized. This history has led me to have the distinct sense that we have been through the "circling back of time" (Gibbs 2005, 199). To baldly paraphrase Hegel, history has been presented as the slow march towards progress, in this case progressive legalization, when in fact it is cyclical (Hegel 1860, 56). This book has presented a (mostly) linear history of the legalization to illustrate this fact. This gloomy thought suggests that people who are seriously interested in progressively legalizing unilateral acts would find it more helpful to break this cycle and to treat these acts as discrete acts. Some of these acts may be foundational of international law, while only a limited number of others may create binding legal obligations. This is the lesson that can be learned from the history of unilateral acts.

Works cited

Abbott, K.W., R.O. Keohane, A. Moravcsik, A.-M. Slaughter, and D. Snidal. 2000. "The Concept of Legalization." *International Organization* 54 (3): 401.

n.d. "Accordance with International Law of the Declaration of Independence in Respect of Kosovo [Advisory Opinion] (July 22, 2010), Declaration of Judge Tomka." *ICJ*. www.icj-cij.org.

n.d. "Accordance with International Law of the Declaration of Independence in Respect of Kosovo [Advisory Opinion] (July 22, 2010), Dissenting Opinion of Judge Koroma."

n.d. "Accordance with International Law of the Declaration of Independence in Respect of Kosovo [Advisory Opinion] (July 22, 2010), Dissenting Opinion of Judge Skotnikov." *ICJ*. www.icj-cij.org.

n.d. "Accordance with International Law of the Declaration of Independence in Respect of Kosovo [Advisory Opinion] (July 22, 2010), Separate Opinion of Judge Bennouna." *ICJ*. www.icj-cij.org.

n.d. "Accordance with International Law of the Declaration of Independence in Respect of Kosovo [Advisory Opinion] (July 22, 2010), Separate Opinion of Judge Cancado-Trinidade." *ICJ*. www.icj-cij.org.

n.d. "Accordance with International Law of the Declaration of Independence in Respect of Kosovo [Advisory Opinion] (July 22, 2010), Separate Opinion of Judge Sepulveda Amor." *ICJ*. www.icj-cij.org.

n.d. "Accordance with International Law of the Declaration of Independence in Respect of Kosovo [Advisory Opinion] (July 22, 2010), Separate Opinion of Judge Yusuf." *ICJ*. www.icj-cij.org.

n.d. Accordance with International Law of the Unilateral Declaration of Independence in Respect of Kosovo (Request for Advisory Opinion). www.icj-cij.org.

n.d. "Accordance with International Law of the Unilateral Declaration of Independence in Respect of Kosovo [Advisory Opinion] (July 22, 2010)." *ICJ*. Accessed July 15, 2013. www.icj-cij.org.

Aegean Sea Continental Shelf Case (Greece v. Turkey) (Judgment). 1978. (ICJ).

Aerial Incident of 10 August 1999 (Pakistan v. India). 2000. (ICJ).

Alvarez, A. 1909. "Latin American International Law." *AJIL* 3 (2): 269.

Anghie, A. 2005. *Imperialism, Sovereignty and the Making of International Law*. Cambridge: CUP.

———. 2006. "The Evolution of International Law: Colonial and Postcolonial Realities." *Third World Quarterly*, 739. n.d. "Autonomy." Oxford English Dictionary Online.

Barrett, J.A. 1928. "The Real Monroe Doctrine." *Transactions of the Grotius Society* 1.

Bassiouni, M. Cherif. 1996. "International Crimes: 'Jus Cogens' and 'Obligatio Erga Omnes'." *L & Contemp Rob* 59 (4): 63.

Baxi, U. 2005. "The 'War on Terror' and the 'War of Terror': Nomadic Multitudes, Aggressive Incumbents, and the 'New' International Law: Prefactory Remarks on Two 'Wars'." *Osgoode Hall LJ* 43: 8.

Becker Lorca, A. 2012. "Eurocentrism in the History of International Law." In *The Oxford Handbook of the History of International Law*, edited by A. Peters and B. Fassbender, 1034–1057. Oxford: OUP.

Benton, L. 2002. *Law and Colonial Cultures: Legal Regimes in World History 1400–1900*. Cambridge: CUP.

Berg, Bruce L. 2009. *Qualitative Research Methods for the Social Sciences*. 7th edition. Boston, MA: Allyn & Bacon.

Bix, B. 2003. *Jurisprudence: Theory and Context*. 3rd edition. London: Sweet & Maxwell.

———. 2004. "Black's Law Dictionary." "Perfect". West.

Bowden, B. 2005. "The Colonial Origins of International Law, European Expansion and the Classical Standard of Civilization." *Journal of the History of International Law* 7: 1.

Bowett, D.W. 1957. "Estoppel Before International Tribunals and Its Relation to Acquiesence." *Brit YB Int'l L* 33: 176.

Brown, C. 1995–1996. "A Comparative and Critical Assessment of Estoppel in International Law." *U Miami L Rev* 50: 369.

Brownlie, I. 1998. *Principles of Public International Law*. 5th edition. Oxford: Clarendon/OUP.

Bulman, T.P., 1999. "A Dangerous Guessing Game Designed as Elightened Policy: United Staets Law of War Obligations During Military Operations Other Than War." *Military L Rev* 159: 152.

Burley, A.-M. 1992. "Toward an Age of Liberal Nations." *Harv Int'l LJ* 33: 393.

Byers, M. 1997. "Conceptualizing the Relationship Between Jus Cogens and Erga Omnes Rules." *Nordic J Int'l L* 66: 211.

Case Concerning Border and Transborder Armed Actions (Nicaragua v. Honduras) (Judgment). 1988. (ICJ).

Case Concerning Delimitation of the Maritime Boundary in the Gulf of Maine Area (Canada v. United States of America). 1984. (ICJ).

2007. "Case Concerning Military and Paramilitary Activities in and Against Nicaragua (Nicaragua v. USA) ICJ Oral Pleadings." *ICJ*. May 31. www.icj-cij.org/docket/files/70/9641.pdf.

n.d. "Case Concerning Military and Paramilitary Activities in and Against Nicaragua (Nicaragua v. Usa) Memorial of Nicaragua (Merits)." *ICJ*. Accessed May 31, 2007. www.icj-cij.org/docket/files/70/9619.pdf.

n.d. "Case Concerning Sovereignty over Pedra Branca/ Pulau Batu Puteh, Middle Rocks and South Ledge (Malaysia v. Singapore) (Judgment) [2008] List No 130." *ICJ*. Accessed June 2, 2009. www.icj-cij.org/docket/files/130/14492.pdf.

n.d. "Case Concerning the Barcelona Traction, Light and Power Company (Belgium v. Spain, Second Phase) Judgment [1970] ICJ Rep 3." *ICJ*. www.icj-cij.org/docket/files/50/5387.pdf.

Case Concerning the Barcelona Traction, Light and Power Company Limited (Belgium v. Spain) [Preliminary Objections]. 1964. (ICJ).

Case Concerning the Frontier Dispute (Burkina Faso v. Mali) (Judgment). 1986. General List 69 (ICJ).

Case Concerning the Land and Maritime Boundaries Between Cameroon and Nigeria (Cameroon v. Nigeria) [Preliminary Objections]. 1998. (ICJ).

Case Concerning the Land, Island and Maritime Frontier Dispute (El Salvador v. Honduras) [Request by Nicaragua to Intervene]. 1990. (ICJ).

Case Concerning the Legality of Use of Force (Serbia and Montenegro v. Canada) [Preliminary Objections]. 2004. (ICJ).

Case Concerning the Temple of Preah Vihear (Merits). 1962. (ICJ).

Cassese, A. 2005. *International Law*. Second. Oxford: OUP.

Chayes, A. 1997. "Sumposium [sic]: Nuclear Weapons, the World Court and Global Security: Living History Interview." *Trans'l L & Contemp Probs* 7: 468–469.

Chimni, B.S. n.d. "Third World Approaches to International Law: A Manifesto." *International Community Law Review* 8: 3.

n.d. "Costa Rica Brings a Case Against Nicaragua to the Court in a Dispute Concerning Navigational and Related Rights of Costa Rica on the San Juan River (Press Release 2005/20)." *ICJ*. Accessed April 1, 2008. www.icj-cij.org.

n.d. "Counter-Memorial of Nicaragua, Dispute Concerning Navigational and Related Rights (Costa Rica v. Nicaragua)."

Craven, M. 2015. "Between Law and History: The Berlin Conference of 1884–1885 and the Logic of Free Trade." *London Review of International Law*, 31.

Daskalovski, Z. 2005. "Claims to Kosovo: Nationalism and Self-Determination." In *Understanding the War in Kosovo*, edited by F. Bieber and Z. Daskalovski, 12. London: Frank Cass/Taylor and Francis.

2009. "Dispute Regarding Navigational and Related Rights (Costa Rica v. Nicaragua) [Judgment]." *ICJ*. July 13. Accessed November 26, 2013. www.icj-cij.org.

Dupuy, P.M. 2000. "The Place and Role of Unilateralism in Contemporary International Law." *EJIL* 11: 19.

Eckhart, C. 2012. *Promises of States Under International Law*. London: Hart.

Encyclopedia Britannica. 2013. "Calvo Doctrine." *Encyclopedia Britannica*. Accessed January 1. www.britannica.com.

Fassbender, B., and Peters, A. 2012. "Introduction: Towards a Global History of International Law." In *The Oxford Hanbook of The History of International Law*, edited by A. Peters, and B. Fassbender, 1–24. Oxford: OUP.

Fidler, D.P. 2000. "A Kinder Gentler System of Capitulations? international Law. Structural Adjustment Policies, and the Standard of Liberal, Globalized Civilization." *Tex Int'l LJ* 35: 387.

Fidler, D.P. 2001. "The Return of the Standard of Civilization." *Chi J Int'l L* 2: 137.

Fiedler, W. 2000. "Unilateral Acts in International Law." In *Encyclopedia of International Law*, edited by R. Bernhardt, P. Macalister-Smith and Max Planck Institute. Vol. 4. Amsterdam; New York: North-Holland.

Fisheries Case (United Kingdom v. Norway). 1951. General List 5 (ICJ, December 18).

Fisheries Juridiction Case (Spain v. Canada) (Judgment -Jurisdiction). 1998. General List No 96 (ICJ).

Fitzmaurice, G., Sir. 1958. "The Law and Procedure of the International Court of Justice 1951–1954: Treaty Interpretation and Other Points." *BYIL* 22: 302.

Franck, T. 1975. "Word Made Law: The Decision of the ICJ in the Nuclear Tests Cases." *AJIL* 69: 612.

Franck, T.M. 1992. "The Emerging Right to Democratic Governance." *AJIL* 86: 46.

Foucault, M. 1990. *The History of Sexuality: Volume 1, an Introduction*. Translated by R Hurley, p 12. New York: Vintage Books.

Garner, J.W. 1933. "The International Binding Force of Unilateral Oral Declarations." *AJIL* 27: 493.

Garner, J.W. 1930. "The Recrudescence of the." *Poli Sci Q* 45 (2): 231.

Gibbs, R. 2005. "Messianic Epistemology: Thesis XV." In *By Walter Benjamin and History*, edited by Andrew Benjamin, 197. New York: Continuum.

Gilderhus, M.T. 2006. "The Monroe Doctrine: Meanings and Implications." *Presidential Studies Quarterly* 36 (1): 5.

Gill, T.D. 1989. "Litigation Strategy in the Nicaragua Case at the International Court." In *International Law at a Time of Perplexity: Essays in Honour Shabtai Rosenne*, edited by Y. Dinstein and M. Taboury. Dordrecht/London: Martinus Nijhof.

Glennon, M.J. 1999. "The New Interventionism: The Search for a Just International Law." *Foreign Affairs* 2.

Gordon, P.E. n.d. "What Is Intellectual History? A Frankly Partisan Introduction to a Frequently Misunderstood Field." Accessed January 16, 2014. http://projects.iq.harvard.edu/files/history/files/what_is_intell_history_pgordon_mar2012.pdf.

Gordon, R.W. 1984. "Critical Legal Histories." *Stanford Law Review* 57: 57.

Guzina, D. 2005. "Kosovo or Kosova -Could It Be Both? The Case of Interlocking Serbian and Albanian Nationalisms." In *Understanding the War in Kosovo*, edited by F. Bieber and Z. Daskalovski, 30. London: Frank Case/Taylor and Francis E-Library.

Hegel, G.F.W. 1860. *Lectures on the Philosophy of History*. 3rd edition. Translated by J. Sibre. London.

Howse, R., and Teitel, R. 2010. "Delphic Dictum: How Has the ICJ Contributed to the Global Rule of Law By Its Ruling on Kosovo." *German L.J.* 11: 841.

Hull, W. 1914. "The Monroe Doctrine, National or International." *Proceedings of the American Society of International Law at Its Annual Meeting* 155.

n.d. "ILC Yearbook 1996." UN.

Inman, S.G. 1921. "The Monroe Doctrine and Hispanic America." *The Hispanic American Historical Review* 4 (4): 635–676.

n.d. "Intent." Concise Oxford English Dictionary.

n.d. "Introduction." *ILC*. Accessed December 10, 2007. http://untreaty.un.org/ilc/ilcintro.htm.

Janis, MW. 2012. "North America: American Exceptionalism in International Law." In *The Oxford Handbook of the History of International Law*, 525–552. Oxford: OUP.

Jennings, R. Sir, and Watts A. Sir. 1996. *Oppenheim's International Law*. 9th edition. Vol. 1. London: Longman Harlwo.

Kasson, J.A. 1881. "The Monroe Doctrine in 1881." *The North American Review* 133 (301): 523.

Kennedy, D. 1987. "The Sources of International Law." *Am U J Int'l L & Pol* 2: 1.

Kennedy, D. 1988–1989. "A New Stream of International Law Scholarship." *Wis Int'l L.J.* 7: 1.

Kennedy, D. 1996. "International Law in the Nineteenth Century: History of an Illusion." *Nordic Journal of International Law* 385.

Kindred H., et al. 1993. *International Law: Chiefly as Interpreted and Applied in Canada*. Toronto: Emond Montgomery.

Koskenniemi, M. 2006. *From Apology to Utopia: The Structure of International Legal Argument. Reissue*. Cambridge: CUP.

Koskenniemi, M. 2002. *The Gentle Civilizer of Nations: The Rise and Fall of International Law 1870–1960*. Cambridge: CUP.

———. 2007. "The Fate of Public International Law: Between Technique and Politics." *MLR* 7 (1): 30.

——— 2012. "Law, Teleology and International Relations: An Essay in Counter-disciplinarity." *IR* 26 (1): 3.

Kruger, Peter. 2012. "From the Paris Peace Treaties to the End of the Second World War." In *The Oxford Handbook of the History of International Law*, edited by A. Peters and B. Fassbender, 679–697. Oxford: OUP.

Kwiatkowska, B. 1995. "New Zealand v. France Nuclear Tests Case: The "Little Big" Order of the International Court of Justice of 22 September 1995." *Ius-Gentium: The Finnish Yearbook of International Law* 6: 1.

Lauterpacht, H. 1927. *Private Law Sources and Analogies of International Law* (with Special Reference to International Arbitration). London: Longmans.

The Law Review of British and Foreign Jurisprudence. 1849. London: Hein.

Legal Status of Eastern Greenland (Denmark v. Norway). n.d. Series A/B No 53 (PCIJ). In *World Court Reports: A Collection of the Judgments Orders and Opinions of the Permanent Court of International Justice*, edited by M.O. Hudson. Vol 3. Carnegie Endowment, Oceana.

MacGibbon, I.C. 1958. "Estoppel in International Law." *ICLQ* 7: 468.

Maritime Dispute (Peru v. Chile), *Judgment of 24 January 2014*. Accessed March 22, 2018. www.icj-cij.org.

Marks, S. 1997. "The End of History? Reflections on Some International Legal Thesis." *EJIL* 3: 449.

McNair, L. 1924. "The Legality of the Occupation of the Ruhr." *British Year Book of International Law* 5: 35

n.d. "Memorial of Costa Rica, Dispute Concerning Navigational and Related Rights (Costa Rica v. Nicaragua)." *ICJ*. Accessed May 5, 2009. www.icj-cij.org/docket/files/133/15084.pdf.

———. 1986. "Military and Paramilitary Activities in and Against Nicaragua (Nicaragua v. United States of America) (Judgment, Merits)." *ICJ*. June 27. Accessed February 20, 2014. www.icj-cij.org/docket/files/70/65-3.pdf.

Mills, K., W.B. Taylor, and S. Lauderdale Graham. 2002. *Colonial Latin America: A Documentary History*. Willmington: S.R. Books.

Monroe, J., President. n.d. "Monroe Doctrine [Seventh Annual Address to Congress] (2 December 1823)." *The Avalon Project*. Accessed November 2, 2007. www1.yale.edu/Avalon/Monroe.htm.

Moore, J.B. 1896. "The Monroe Doctrine." *Pol Sci Q* 11: 1.

1930. "More Talk About the Monroe Doctrine." *Advocate of Peace Through Justice* 92 (3): 153.

n.d. National Membership of the League of Nations. Accessed June 20, 2017. www.indiana.edu/~league/nationalmember.htm.

2017. National Security Strategy of the United States of America (December 2017). December 18. Accessed January 22, 2018. www.whitehouse.gov/wp-content/uploads/2017/12/NSS-Final-12-18-2017-0905.pdf.

Neff, Stephen C. n.d. "A Short History Of International Law." In *International Law*, edited by M.C. Evans, 3. Oxford: OUP.

North Sea Continental Shelf Case (Denmark v. Federal Republic of Germany/Netherland v. Federal Republic of Germany). 1969. (ICJ).

n.d. "Nuclear Tests (Australia v. France) Memorial on Jurisdiction and Admissibility Submitted by the Government of Australia." *ICJ*. Accessed May 31, 2007. www.icj-cij.org/docket/files/58/9443.pdf.

n.d. "Nuclear Tests (Australia v. France) Oral Arguments on Jurisdication and Admissiblity: Minutes of Public Sittings." *ICJ*. Accessed May 31, 2007. http://icj-cij.org/docket/files/58/11829.pdf.

Nuclear Tests (Australia v. France), Dissenting Opinion, Judge De Castro (Judgment). 1974. General List 58 (ICJ).

Nuclear Tests (Australia v. France), Dissenting Opinion, Judge Sir Garfield Barwick (Judgment). 1974. General List 58 (ICJ).

Nuclear Tests (Australia v. France) Separate Opinion of Judge Gros (Judgment). 1974. General List 58 (ICJ).

n.d. "Nuclear Tests (New Zealand v France) Memorial on Jurisdiction and Admissiblity Submitted by the Government of New Zeland." *ICJ*. Accessed May 31, 2007. http://icj-cij.org/docket/files/59/9451.pdf.

Nuclear Tests (New Zealand v. France) Dissenting Opinion, Judge Sir Garfield Barwick (Judgment). 1974. General List 59 (ICJ).

Nuclear Tests (New Zealand v. France) Joint Dissenting Opinion (Judgment). 1974. General List 59 (ICJ).

n.d. "Nuclear Tests (New Zealand v. France) Oral Arguments on Jursidction and Admissibility: Public Sittings." *ICJ*. Accessed May 31, 2007. http://icj-cij.org/docket/files/59/9453.pdf.

Nuclear Tests Case (Australia v. France) (Judgment). 1974. General List 58 (ICJ).

Nuclear Tests Case (New Zeland v. France) (Judgment). 1974. General List 59 (ICJ).

O'Connor, J.F. 1991. *Good Faith in International Law*. Dartmouth: Aldershot.

Okafor, O.C. 2005. "Newness, Imperialism, and International Legal Reform in Our Time: A TWAIL Perspective." *Osgoode Hall LJ* 43 (1): 171.

Pahuja, S. 2005. "The Postcoloniality of International Law." *Harv Int'l LJ* 46: 459.

Pahuja, S. 2011. *Decolonizing International Law: Development, Economic Growth and the Politics of Universality*. Cambridge: CUP.

Paris, R. 2002. "International Peacebuilding and 'mission civilatrice'." *Rev of Int'l Stud* 28: 637.

Pellet, A. 1988–1989. "The Normative Dilemma: Will and Consent in International Law Making." *Aust YBIL* 12: 22.

Peters, A. 2011. "Does Kosovo Lie in the Lotus-Land of Freedom?" *Leiden J Int'l L* 24: 95.

n.d. Public Sitting Held on Tuesday 31 May, 2011, at 10 am, at the Peace Palace, President Owada Presiding in the Request for Interpretation of the Judgment of 15 June 1962 in the Case Concerning the Temple of Preah Vihear (Cambodia v. Thailand) (Cambodia v. Thailand). www.icj-cij.org.

Ragazzi, M. 2000. *The Concept of International Obligations Erga Omnes*. Oxford: OUP.

Rajgopal, B. 2003. *International Law From Below: Development, Social Movements and Third World Resistance*. Cambridge: CUP.

Reisman, W.M. 1990. "Editorial Comment: International Law After the Cold War." *AJIL* 84 (4): 859.

Reisman, W.M. 2002. "Unratified Treaties and Other Unperfected Acts in International Law: Constitutional Functions." *Vand J Transnat'l L* 35: 729.

n.d. "Report of the Internaional Law Commission on the Work of its Fifty-Fifth Session (2003) UN DOC A/58/10, Supplement 10." *ILC*. http://untreaty.un.org/ilc/reports/2003/2003report.htm.

2005. "Report of the International Law Commission on the Work of its Fifty-Second Session (2000) UN DOC A/55/10, Supplment No 10." *ILC*. June 2005. http://daccessdds.un.org/doc/UNCOC/GEN/N))/644/24/IMG/N0066424.pdf?openelement.

n.d. "Report of the International Law Commission on the Work of Fifty-First Session (1999) UN DOC A/54/10, Supplement 10." Accessed June 29, 2005. www.un.org/law/ilc/reports/1999/english/99refra.htm.

n.d. "Report of the International Law Commission on the Work of its Fiftieth Session (1998) UNDOC A/53/10, Supplement 10." *ILC*. Accessed June 29, 2005. www.un.org/law/ilc/reports/1998/98repfra.htm.

n.d. "Report of the International Law Commission on the Work of its Fiftieth-Second Session (2000) UN DOC A/55/10, Supplement 10." *ILC*. www.un.org/law/ilc.

n.d. "Report of the International Law Commission on the Work of its Fifty-Eight Session (2006) UN DOC A/61/10, Supplement 10." *ILC*. Accessed May 7, 2007. http://daccessdds.un.org/UNDOC/GEN.NO6/496/47/PDF/NO649647.pdf?OpenElement.

n.d. "Report of the International Law Commission on the Work of its Fifty-Fourth Session (2002) UN DOC A/57/10 Supplement 10." *ILC*. Accessed June 29, 2005. www.un.org/law/ilc/reports/2002/2002report.htm.

n.d. "Report of the International Law Commission on the Work of its Fifty-Sixth Session (2004) UN DOC A/59/10, Supplment 10." *ILC*. Accessed June 17, 2008. http://untreaty.un.oorg/ilc/reports/2004/2004report.htm.

n.d. "Report of the International Law Commission on the Work of its Fifty-Third Session (2001) UN DOC A/56/10, supplement 10." *ILC*. Accessed June 29, 2005. www.un.org/law/ilc/reports/2001/2001report.htm.

n.d. "Report of the International Law Commission on the Work of its Forty-Ninth Session (1997)." *UN*. www.un.org/law/ilc.

n.d. "Request for Intepretation of the Judgment of June 15, 1962 in the Case Concerning the Temple of Preah Vihear (Cambodia v. Thailand) (Cambodia v. Thailand) [Judgment] (November 11, 2013)." *ICJ*. www.icj-cij.org.

n.d. "Request for Interpretation of the Judgment of 15 June 1962 in the Case of the Temple of Preah Vihear (Cambodia v. Thailand) [Cambodia v. Thailand] [Application Instituting Proceedings]." *ICJ*. www.icj-cij.org.

1997. "Resolution Adopted by the General Assembly [On the Report of the International Law Commission on the Work of Its Forty-Eight Session, UN DOC UNGA A/Res 51/160." *ILC*. January 30. Accessed June 13, 2013. www.un.org/law/ilc.

n.d. "Resolution Adopted by the General Assembly [on the Report of the UN Sixth Committee A/61/454." UNGA.

Roach, K., P. Healy, and G. Trotter. n.d. *Criminal Law and Procedure: Cases and Materials*. 9th edition. Toronto: Emond Montgomery.

Robertson, W.S. 1918. "The Recognition of the Hispanic American Nations By the United States." *Hispanic American Historical Review* 1 (3): 239.

Rodriguez Cedeno, V. n.d.a. "Second Report on the Unilateral Acts of States (1999) UN DOC A/CN.4/500."

———. n.d.b. "Sixth Report on Unilateral Acts of States by Victor Rodriguez Cedeno Special Rapporteur (2003) UN DOC A/CN.4/534."

Rogel, C. 2003. "Kosovo: Where It All Began." *International Journal of Politics, Culture and Society* 17 (1): 167.

Root, E. 1914. "The Real Monroe Doctrine." *AJIL* 8: 427.

Roskin, M. 1974. "From Pearl Harbor to Vietnam: Shifting Generational Paradigns and Foreign Policy." *Political Science Quarterly* 89 (3): 563.

Rubin, A. 2001. "Actio Popularis, Jus Cogens and Offences Erga Omnes." *New England L Rev* 35 (2): 265.

Rubin, A.P. 1977. "The International Effects of Unilateral Declarations." *AJIL* 71: 1.

Rubin, E. 1998. "The Practice and Discourse of Legal Scholarship." *Mich L Rev* 86: 1835.

Saganek, P. 2015. *Unilateral Acts of States in Public International Law*. Leiden/Boston, MA: Brill/Nijhoff.

Schwarzenberger, G. 1955. "The Fundamental Principles of International Law." *Rec Des Cours*. 195.

Shaw, M.N. 1997. *International Law*. Cambridge: CUP.

———. 2008. *International Law*. 6th edition. Cambridge: CUP.

Sheppard, W.R. 1924. "The Monroe Doctrine Reconsidered." *Poli Sci Q* 39 (1): 35.

Simmons, J.F. 1907. "The Monroe Doctrine: Its Status." *Mich L Rev* 5 (4): 236.

South African History Online. n.d. "General Act of the Berlin Conference on West Africa, 26 February, 1885." Accessed December 11, 2017. www.sahistory.org.za/archive/general-act-berlin-conference-west-africa-26-february-1885.

Spencer, J.H. 1936. "The Monroe Doctrine and the League Covenant." *AJIL* 30 (3): 400.
Stern, J. 2015. "Obama and Terrorism: Like It or Not the War Goes On." Foreign Affairs, September–October.
Stone, J. 2017. Catalonia's Independence: How Did It Happen? A Timeline of Key Events. October 27. Accessed January 23, 2018. www.independent.co.uk/news/world/europe/catalonia-independence-what-happened-spain-timeline-events-referendum-latest-a8023711.html.
Tams, C.J. 2005. *Enforcing Obligations Erga Omnes in International Law*. Cambridge: CUP.
Tams, C.J., and A. Asteriti. 2013. "Erga Omnes, Jus Cogens, and Their Impact on the Law of Responsibility." In *International Responsibility of* the *European Union*, edited by M. Evans and P. Koutrakos. London: Hart.
The Case of the SS Lotus. 1927. Ser A No 10 (PCIJ).
n.d. "The Charter of the United Nations, adopted 26 June 1945, Entry Into Force 24 October 1945 UKTS 1946, No 67." *UN*. Accessed December 10, 2007. www.un.org/aboutun/charter.
n.d. "The Covenant of the League of Nations." *Avalon Project*. Accessed January 31, 2014. http://avalon.yale.edu.
Thirlway, H. 2010. "The Sources of International Law." In *Intnerational Law*, edited by M.D Evans. Oxford: OUP.
Thirlway, H.W.A. 1990. "The Law and Procedure of the International Court of Justi e 1960–1989." *BYIL* 60: 1.
Thomas-Peter, H. 2018. *Sky News*. January 21. Accessed January 22, 2018. https://news.sky.com/story/former-un-ambassador-samantha-power-criticises-donald-trumps-foreign-policy-11216542.
Tower, C. 1920. "The Origin and Meaning of the Monroe Doctrine." *AJIL* 1.
n.d. "Unilateral Acts of States: Replies from Governments to the Questionnaire: Report of the Secretary General [2000] UNGA Doc A/CN.4/511." *UNGA*. http://daccessdds.un.org/doc/UNDOC/GEN/N00/520/46/PDF/N0052046.pdf?OpenElement.
Vec, M. 2012. "From the Congress of Vienna to the Parice Peace Treaties for 1919." In *The Oxford Handbook of the History of International Law*, edited by A. Peters and B. Fassbender, 654–678. Oxford: OUP.
Vermeer-Kunzli, A. 2007. "A Matter of Interest: Diplomatic Protection and State Responsibility Erga Omnes." *ICLQ* 56 (3): 554.
Verzijil, J.H.W. 1973. *International Law in Historical Perspective*. Leiden: AW Sijthoff.
Wagner, M.L. 1986. "Jursidiction by Estoppel in the International Court of Justice." *Calif L Rev* 74: 1778.
Westlake, J. 1984. *Chapters on the Principles of International Law as Quoted in Anghie, Evolution*. Cambridge: CUP.
———. 1910. *International Law*. Vol. 2. 2 vols. Cambridge: CUP.
———. 1910. *International Law*. Vol. 1. 2 vols. Cambridge: CUP.
———. n.d. "Will." Concise Oxford English Dictionary Online.
Wright, Q. 1970. "How Hostilities Have Ended: Peace Treaties and Alternatives." *Annals of the American Academy of Political Science* 51.
Yasuaki, O. 2000. "When Was the Law of International Society Born? An Inquiry of the History of International Law from an Intercivilizational Perspective." *Journal of the History of International Law* 2: 54.

n.d. "Yearbook of the International Law Commission 1997 Vol 11 (Part Two)." *ILC.* Accessed June 13, 2013. www.un.org/law/ilc.

n.d. "Yearbook of the International Law Commission, Vol 1 [1997] UNGA Doc A/CN.L.543." ILC.

n.d. "Yearbook of the International Law Commission, Vol 2 [1998] UNGA Doc A/53/10." ILC. Accessed June 29, 2007. http://untreaty.un.org/ilc/guide/gfra.htm.

Yin, R.K. 2011. *Qualitative Research from Start to Finish.* New York: Guilford Press.

Zucchino, D. 2017. Does the Kurdish Dream of Independence Have a Chance? September 30. Accessed January 23, 2018. www.nytimes.com/2017/09/30/world/middleeast/kurds-iraq-independence.html.

Index

For Product Safety Concerns and Information please contact our EU representative GPSR@taylorandfrancis.com
Taylor & Francis Verlag GmbH, Kaufingerstraße 24, 80331 München, Germany

www.ingramcontent.com/pod-product-compliance
Ingram Content Group UK Ltd.
Pitfield, Milton Keynes, MK11 3LW, UK
UKHW021958180926
475701UK00003B/79

9780367590383